Barbara H. Kuzich

FROM CRADLE
TO GRAVE

FROM CRADLE
TO GRAVE

The Human Face
of Poverty in America

Jonathan Freedman

Atheneum
New York
1993

Maxwell Macmillan Canada
Toronto

Maxwell Macmillan International
New York   Oxford   Singapore   Sydney

Copyright © 1993 by Jonathan Freedman

Atheneum   Maxwell Macmillan Canada, Inc.
Macmillan Publishing Company   1200 Eglinton Avenue East
866 Third Avenue   Suite 200
New York, NY 10022   Don Mills, Ontario M3C 3N1

Macmillan Publishing Company is part of the Maxwell Communication
Group of Companies.

Library of Congress Cataloging-in-Publication Data
Freedman, Jonathan L.
    From cradle to grave / by Jonathan Freedman.
      p.   cm.
    Includes index.
    ISBN 0-689-12126-1
    1. Poor—United States. 2. Family—United States. 3. Problem solv-
ing. 4. Social problems—United States. 5. Poverty—United States.
I. Title.
    HV4045.F74   1993   93–7708
    362.5'0973—dc20   CIP

Macmillan books are available at special discounts for bulk purchases
for sales promotions, premiums, fund-raising, or educational use. For
details, contact:

Special Sales Director
Macmillan Publishing Company
866 Third Avenue
New York, NY 10022

10 9 8 7 6 5 4 3 2 1

Printed in the United States of America

BIRTH IS A BEGINNING

Birth is a beginning
And death a destination
And life is a journey:
From childhood to maturity
And youth to age;
From innocence to awareness
And ignorance to knowing;
From foolishness to discretion
     And then, perhaps, to wisdom;
From weakness to strength
Or strength to weakness—
     And, often, back again;
From health to sickness
     And back, we pray, to health again;
From offense to forgiveness,
From loneliness to love,
From joy to gratitude,
From pain to compassion,
And grief to understanding—
     From fear to faith;
From defeat to defeat to defeat—
Until, looking backward or ahead,
We see that victory lies
Not at some high place along the way,
But in having made the journey, stage by stage,
     A sacred pilgrimage.
Birth is a beginning
And death a destination.
And life is a journey,
A sacred pilgrimage—
     To life everlasting.

—ALVIN I. FINE
A prayer for Yom Kippur in
The Gates of Repentance

CONTENTS

FROM CRADLE
TO GRAVE

THE PERILOUS JOURNEY

At every stage of life's journey, Americans are falling by the wayside into poverty. Yet we have no comprehensive vision of how poverty relates to human development, no sense of how to help people struggling to make it through their lives. Consequently, and tragically, there is no life-sustaining support network to prevent Americans from falling into permanent poverty—or to make their way out of it.

My goal in writing this book was to learn how people cope with the most destructive deprivations, and see how some manage to survive, grow, and thrive. Visiting prenatal clinics, schools, job-training centers, and nursing homes, I asked people to share their knowledge: What helps, what hurts, what works?

I consciously sought out people who had conquered severe problems, and explored programs that helped them. The goal was not to give a falsely rosy picture of life in America, but to show that even the worst problems may be dealt with—and that we can learn from our successes.

Their lives have much to teach us, but their voices have largely been shut out of the poverty debate dominated by economists, politicians, and social scientists. My bias should be clear from the beginning: I find simple life stories more persuasive than brilliant, abstract arguments. Lives reflect realities that are far more complex than the narrow issues that so often result in unworkable and inhumane policies.

This book advances chronologically through the stages of life, with chapters devoted to prenatal development, infancy, early childhood, school age, adolescence, family, mid-life, aging and dying—and a conclusion of policy recommendations. Each chapter could be a book, and specialists in each field are qualified to fill in the gaps that I have left.

I consciously chose to frame this issue in a life-span perspective because I believe it is important to grasp the whole scope of poverty, not just the parts. Asking how ordinary people overcome extraordinary obstacles provides insights that lie outside the frame of the polarized poverty debate. This book explores the relationship between the stages of life and how problems mount—and how preventive and healing strategies affect people along the way.

It is about middle-class adults who plunge into poverty, as well as babies doomed to deprivation from the moment of conception. I do not believe a wall separates "us," the supposedly secure, from "them," the so-called underclass. Social problems pervade all classes, races, and ages; the breakdown of institutions and relationships threatens all Americans.

As my research progressed, I began to see life as a staircase, and each stage as a stair step. The risers are the tasks people must accomplish before moving forward. Because I could not find a single person or family going through all the stages, I selected different people and families from around the country whose life dramas brought home the issues. The similarities I found among people from widely different backgrounds made it seem, ultimately, that I was writing about an extended family— the American people.

Family is the hub of the life span. The new norm is that most American marriages split up; the center of our society is coming apart. Families are crucial to helping people survive, grow, and develop, but no particular family style is universal. The best approach is to let families define themselves, listen to their needs, and support them as they struggle to accomplish their goals.

My method was to find programs that were successful and seek out people who had been helped by them. I searched for success stories because I wanted to know how people succeeded against all odds, and what their stories could teach.

As a journalist focusing on social issues for more than a decade, I grew frustrated writing about people who were "falling through the cracks"* at every age, without presenting a comprehensive approach to help them. Their problems seemed isolated, and my suggestions seemed piecemeal: Support this program, end this policy, don't cut funding. . . . Without a larger context, it seemed futile.

Shifting from daily journalism to this three-year project, I struggled for a larger vision that would put these programs and policies in a meaningful context. One that would be helpful for people not at only one stage, but throughout the journey.

The plight of America's poor, and the vulnerability of the middle class, grows more severe each year. By 1992, the U.S. Bureau of the Census reported that 37.5 million people had fallen below the poverty line—the highest level in twenty-seven years, since the start of President Lyndon Johnson's War on Poverty in 1964.

---

* Americans commonly speak of "falling through the cracks," but the image defies literal definition. Instead, people seem to visualize cracks as gaps in our economic and social systems, or as holes in the so-called safety net.

Jack London described poverty as an "abyss" in *People of the Abyss,* a nonfiction account of the slums of London in 1903.

Suffering is now disproportionately concentrated among young people left out of the political process: Forty percent of the poor are children, four times the proportion of elderly. Although this huge poverty gap between the two age groups is largely due to massive government spending for the elderly in comparison to meager handouts to children, the dominant myth in American politics over the past decade was that government programs didn't work.

The fragility of families living on the edge was brought home by events that have happened to my own family. During the writing of this book, the afternoon newspaper where I had won the Pulitzer prize died; the British company that owned my prestigious American book publisher went into court protection; the insurance company that held policies for my children's college education went belly-up and had to be rescued by the state; our uninsured medical expenses soared; the savings and loan that sold me my first mortgage went bankrupt; the flagship state university where I taught journalism threatened to close key departments and fire 147 tenured professors; even my children's magnet school suffered cutbacks and had to dispense with the reading teacher, counselor, and sex education program, while AIDS was on the rise among teenagers.

Luckily, we remain healthy, intact, and solvent, but as I interviewed Americans who lost their jobs, their health, their homes, their security, it was not hard to identify with them.

Some of the people in this book wished to be known by their real names; others only spoke on the condition that their names be withheld. For them I invented new names, and, in some cases, changed minor details to protect their privacy. It is courageous for people to share their private dramas publicly; many hope their problems will prevent others from making the same mistakes. Some have done cruel things, often repeating patterns of abuse they experienced as children. I do not intend to judge these individuals, for no one's life is spotless, but to use these stories to portray larger issues.

Although President Bill Clinton has promised rapid action on jobs, health care, and welfare reform, powerful interests oppose change. This book takes a long-term view of poverty; its recommendations, hopefully, will provide a broader framework for action not only in the coming years, but over the next decades.

My objective is to show what we can do as a nation to make the journey more secure and less destructive. In simple terms, it's about building a railing up the stairway. A railing is not a safety net that catches people after they've fallen all the way down to poverty, nor is it a bootstrap by which they supposedly pull themselves up. A railing is used to prevent falls and to guide people upward; it makes ascent safer without taking away self-reliance. The railing I envision is anchored by some government programs, but it's also made up of community and private efforts; in the end, I imagine it as a railing formed of human hands.

As this project progressed, I came to love and respect the people who shared their secrets with me. They have written this book with their lives, and it is dedicated to them.

PRENATAL

ONE CLEAN BABY

Two babies are conceived in America; one in liberty, the other in addiction. Even before birth, the blank slates of their lives are scarred with the graffiti of the drug culture, or endangered by the fine print of a health-insurance policy.

How these and millions of other American babies grow up will in part determine whether America will grow, or fail to thrive, in the next century. The historic pattern of this nation's economic growth—ever expanding and growing in size, power, and wealth—is being called into question as our economy falters, our frontiers shrink, our domestic infrastructure rusts, and our family structure breaks apart. This pattern of decline threatens the physical, mental, and social development of America's children.

Yet, in a hopeful way, these children's struggle to be born healthy and develop to their full potential reveals a new path for America's growth and development. In this new path, growth may be less like a cancer—mindless expansion that crowds out and ultimately kills healthy organisms—and more like the unfolding of an individual human life through the stages of development, from microscopic sperm and egg to the fullness of age.

The mothers of these two unborn babies are a portrait in the contrasts of America in the 1990s. Kenya Williams is a young, unmarried black woman whose first child was born high on crack and never lived to see his second day. At the onset of her second pregnancy, Kenya is living with a crack pusher in San Diego and remains addicted to cocaine. Cindy Miller is a white, middle-class college graduate living in Wabash, Indiana. Beginning her second pregnancy, she has a healthy sixteen-month-old boy, a good job with health coverage, and a strong marriage.

The children they have conceived will be among the 4 million born every year in the United States. They are the children who, in a civilized society like ours, one expects will crawl, toddle, and run headlong into the twenty-first century.

But the facts alone in these two cases point to different expectations for the lives of these children; and the facts, with all of their complexities, point to the vacant heart, the deep contradictions in our country.

I met Kenya in a peer-group session at Options for Recovery, an experimental drug-treatment program for pregnant women, in August 1990. When I entered the windowless room where thirty women sat in a circle, I was struck by their eyes, inquisitive and wounded. They wore sweat clothes, jeans, or maternity suits; their hair was brushed but not done up, and few wore makeup. Although some of them showed telltale signs of drugs— tracks in their arms, tattooed and emaciated bodies— most looked like average suburban mothers you'd find shopping for groceries in the middle of the day. They smelled faintly of baby food and perspiration like workers in a day-care center, and through the thin walls, I could hear the faint cries of their children. In that windowless room, maternal warmth radiated from their scarred and tattooed bodies like the sun burning through fog.

The women were awarding each other plastic stickers

embossed with slogans for the number of days they had stayed clean. Although they laughed self-consciously about the corny stickers, the battle each was waging was dead serious, and this showed by their heartfelt appreciation of each other's small victories. One by one, they recounted their feelings of anger, fear, guilt, and hunger for drugs. Through the stories they shared, I learned that, for these women, growing up in suburban homes that appeared stable was a nightmare of abuse that had driven many to escape in demeaning sexual encounters, self-mutilation, and numbing drugs. The poverty many experienced was not economic but emotional deprivation. As children, they had experienced terrible absences of parental love; their feelings of trust, security, and self-worth had been crushed; the sanctity of their own bodies was violated.

I was drawn to a woman who sat apart from the others, one of two blacks among the predominantly white and Latina women. Her stomach wasn't showing, and I wondered if she were pregnant or had already delivered a baby. She spoke quickly and seemed assured of herself, almost too sure. When one of the other women made a joking confession, her taut laughter penetrated to the core, almost like a cry.

I approached her during art therapy. She told me her name was Kenya Williams and she was six weeks pregnant. While the other mothers cut and pasted trite "Gerber baby" pictures, Kenya clipped icy blond vamps from the pages of *Vogue*. She sarcastically called her collage "American Beauty." As she worked, she told me her first baby, exposed to crack in her womb, died two hours after being born. She said it in a matter-of-fact way, mentioning that it happened on a particular day in August. Her face froze. Today was August 19, the first anniversary of her baby's death.

She laid her head on the table. Tears leaked through the chinks in her clenched eyes and dripped on the collage, staining "American Beauty." She released a cold cry. The women turned from their collages. She screamed again, louder. The women froze, turning inward. The next scream seemed to rise from the depths of her womb. A friend went to Kenya's side, putting her arms around her. As the scream died down, Kenya began to moan, rocking rhythmically as if in labor. The other women bent over, clutching their stomachs. The director came in and took Kenya to her office to comfort her.

Exactly one year before, when Kenya went to the University of California San Diego Medical Center complaining of a sharp pain in her lower back, she did not know that she was going to deliver a baby. The emergency room doctor thought she might be passing a kidney stone and admitted her for tests. Kenya knew that she was pregnant, but she did not connect the pain in her back to the child in her womb. Detachment and denial are common characteristics of cocaine—and all other—addictions.

In the back of her mind, Kenya knew something was wrong with her pregnancy: Three months earlier, she had noticed fluid leaking into her underwear. But she blocked out her anxieties by smoking more cocaine, and she never went to the doctor or had a prenatal checkup. Although she had no health insurance, she could have applied for Medicaid; but she was too strung out on crack to bother, and no outreach program made prenatal care easily available.

What was more real to her than the life growing within her womb was the difficulty coping with her parents' disapproval of her boyfriend, and her own disappointment that she'd thrown away her career in computers for cocaine. Finally, her boyfriend's arrest on drug charges triggered her back pain. She came into the hospital with fever approaching 104 degrees, asking for painkillers. After examining her more closely, doctors disregarded the kidney-stone diagnosis and concluded that she had an infected uterus. But by that time, her fetus was seven months old and Kenya had begun premature labor.

"One of you will die," a nurse told Kenya.

She was so despondent that she didn't care. At 11:30 the nurse gave her a painkiller and she fell into a fitful sleep. Sweating heavily, she was awakened by sharp, rapid contractions. She vaguely heard a nurse say, "I think she's going to deliver." They rolled her into the delivery room, and she remained there all night. The baby, a boy, was born the next morning, August 19. When Kenya saw her firstborn child, she was still so strung out that she would later describe him with cruel detachment; he looked "kind of small" and resembled her lover.

"Do you want to hold him?" a delivery nurse asked. Kenya shook her head no. A premonition told her not to touch his little body, even though his heart was beating. Given Kenya's response, the nurse did not wash the baby or wrap him in a blanket; instead, she just left him beneath warming lights on top of the incubator near his oblivious, sleeping mother.

Two hours later, the nurse came in to waken her. "What do you want to do about funeral arrangements?" she asked, holding the baby. Seeing that he was still breathing, Kenya was shocked by the question; but looking closer at her son's small body, she saw he wasn't fully formed. They took him away.

The official cause of death was listed as "immature

gestational stage," but the real cause was crack cocaine. It had interfered with the fetus's attachment to the wall of its mother's uterus; the placenta withered and separated, cutting off oxygen and nutrition and finally infecting the fetus. The baby's organs never developed sufficiently to support life.

Kenya was not charged with murder, or any crime, for the death of her son, although some call for such punishments of crack mothers. Her fallopian tubes were not tied to prevent another pregnancy, and she was not required to have a birth-control implant, as a judge required in the controversial 1991 case of a California mother with a history of child abuse. She was not forced to take personal responsibility for what she had done to her innocent child. Nor was she given drug counseling or help to deal with her guilt and pain. Kenya plunged into depression and medicated herself with illegal drugs.

Every day in America, more than a thousand babies are born, like Kenya's firstborn son, exposed to illegal drugs in the womb. Some infants clench tiny fists and writhe in withdrawal from stimulants; others lie drugged and despondent from narcotics. Many suffer permanent brain, liver, kidney, heart, and lung damage or are twisted with terrible deformities because their mothers shot, sniffed, smoked, or drank to excess. A congressional committee estimated that in one year (1988) of the crack epidemic, 375,000 babies were exposed as fetuses to illegal drugs—that is one in eleven American babies whose basic human rights to healthy development are violated before birth. Over the course of a decade, this means that nearly 4 million American babies will begin life disabled to some degree by drugs—babies who will have to carry this burden for a lifetime as they struggle to achieve critical stages of development.

*   *   *

While the crack epidemic was cutting its devastating swath through America's urban poor throughout the 1980s, the middle class, shielded by the initial prosperity of the Reagan-Bush era, hardly noticed. The credit and borrowing orgy released by Reaganomics puffed up the middle class's life-style so that they felt more secure than at any time since the Eisenhower days. Consequently, most Americans believed that the kinds of tragedies befalling Kenya Williams and her first baby happened only to the so-called underclass, the undeserving poor; and few believed that recovery programs worked.

Middle Americans who worked hard, followed the rules, paid mortgages, and bought health insurance felt somewhat shielded from the traumas and insecurities they saw displayed, with increasing intensity, on their streets and television screens. In fact, if anything, many felt personally endangered by people who committed senseless crimes of violence while on drugs. Many felt taken advantage of by having to support single mothers on welfare. Throughout the eighties, politicians understood this resentment and translated it into support for dismantling the "safety net," program by program: Officials cut taxes, slashed welfare benefits, all the while spending more money on defense abroad, police and prisons at home.

These shifts created a devastating imbalance in the amount of health resources available to people at different stages of the life span. By 1990, the federal government spent, on average, $11,350 for every American over age 65, but spent only $1,020 for every child under age 18, according to the House Ways and Means Committee. The result was a shortage of health resources not only for crack babies, but for children of the middle class.

*   *   *

Wabash, Indiana, home of Cindy Miller, was insulated by sturdy Midwestern grain, cattle, and hog farms, and by the temperament of its 1,800 residents, from the wind-shearing social forces that tore through urban America during the eighties. The Hoosier State, home state of Vice-President Dan Quayle, was by tradition a Republican stronghold of conservative moral values and strong families.

Cindy had worked her way through college and was proud of her position as public relations director for a hospital in Wabash. Her husband, Tim, was a self-employed carpetlayer who was building a small business. Absorbed in her marriage, work, and community, Cindy was vaguely aware of seeing crack mothers and people without health insurance parade their difficulties on television talk shows, but she felt insulated from their harsh world.

The young married couple had waited five years for their first baby, and everything went normally at the beginning. Throughout her pregnancy, Cindy meticulously followed her doctor's orders: no smoking or drinking, a healthy diet, plenty of sleep. Her body became a vessel whose sole purpose was to ensure the healthy development of her baby.

But in her fifth month a severe pain began to cramp her leg, worsening every day. Finally, she went to the emergency room. As the nurse was reading her blood pressure, Cindy watched her face fall with the mercury as her blood pressure plunged to a dangerously low level. Cindy panicked, fearing for her child's life—and her own.

As Tim tried to comfort her, their family practitioner, Dr. Charles Lyons, told her she had phlebitis: inflammation of a vein. Because of hormones released during pregnancy, phlebitis was especially dangerous to a pregnant woman. A clot might form in Cindy's leg and travel to her heart, lodge there, and kill her.

To dissolve the clot, Dr. Lyons gave her heparin, an organic blood thinner that would not endanger the baby. It had to be administered through an IV that would stay in her wrist for the next three months. With this treatment, there was hope that she could have the baby.

Heparin was expensive, about $1,000 a month, but Cindy got it below cost through hospital channels. In any case, the Millers were covered by her $250,000 per-person hospital-employee health insurance policy, so there was little to worry about, provided Cindy's body continued responding to the heparin. They were thankful for their doctor, for their insurance, for their family and, especially, for each other.

When the baby came nearly a month late, Cindy needed no medication. She and Tim worked together as the baby's head crested, followed by a tiny shoulder, then his body—giving birth to a new life. After routine checking, Dr. Lyons placed Cindy's newborn son on his mother's stomach. Nicholas Miller weighed more than eight pounds. His skin, flushed from birth, was deep brown. "Like Martin Luther King," one nurse joked, since that day, January 18, happened to be Martin Luther King Day.

Martin Luther King, Jr., was a childhood hero of Kenya Williams. By her upbringing, Kenya was not an obvious candidate for becoming addicted to crack cocaine and falling through the cracks in America's race-divided society.

Born on Christmas Eve in 1961, she grew up in a black middle-class neighborhood of San Diego, with wispy palms and ranch-style homes set behind emerald-green lawns. Her father graduated from San Diego State University and held a job in the aerospace industry. Her mother stayed home to raise her five children—four daughters and a son—and never permitted alcohol, cigarettes, loud music, or drugs in her home.

Kenya was the third of four daughters: One of her sisters is now a computer consultant; the other two are in college. Her younger brother, a college football star, is studying law. None of her siblings ever had a drug problem. She was among the first students to be bused in San Diego's voluntary desegregation program, and she attended highly regarded integrated schools from third grade through high school.

But Kenya says her seemingly normal middle-class upbringing was overshadowed by bloody beatings with switches. Fruit trees grew in her backyard, and she recalls her mother cutting switches from plum, lemon, lime, nectarine, and peach trees to discipline children who didn't obey, as her mother's father had beaten her when she was a child, as his father had beaten him, and so on back to slave days, when blacks were whipped by their white masters. Knobby plum branches made the most painful switches, and Kenya was the child who got the worst beatings from her mother, beginning in kindergarten and continuing through fifth grade. Many of the beatings related to her conduct in school. She was the class clown, always acting up to get attention, and if she got reprimanded by a teacher, she came home to find the plum switches lying on her bed. Then the ritual beating began.

As Kenya describes it, her mother first made her strip to her panties, then lie facedown on the bed. Raising her arm and her angry voice, Kenya's mother beat Kenya from her neck to her feet. The switch slashed her skin; writhing, she kicked and screamed, rolling onto her back, and the switch struck the front of her body. The beatings seemed eternal but lasted about twenty minutes, until her mother was too exhausted to raise her hand. The next day Kenya would wear long-sleeved shirts and tights to hide the scabs and wounds, but no one ever investigated, she says, because in the 1960s corporal punishment wasn't considered child abuse.

Kenya was introduced to drugs in seventh grade in a gully behind the playground of Dana Junior High, where a group of girls was smoking marijuana. In tenth grade, Kenya graduated from marijuana to PCP, a horse tranquilizer that causes hallucinations. Despite her drug dependency, Kenya's native intelligence and gift for math helped her graduate from Point Loma High School with her class in 1979. She enrolled in Mesa Community College, hoping to become a registered nurse. But PCP interfered with her ability to study and she dropped out of college in 1983.

Kenya brushed off her academic failure and dreamed of earning enough money to leave her parents' house; they were cramping her style. She landed a word-processing job and developed a faculty for decoding complex computer software. Soon she was getting pay raises and job offers from banks and high-tech corporations. She rented a one-bedroom apartment in East San Diego, bought a brand-new Honda Accord, and shopped for clothes at Nordstrom. She began leading a double life. At work she pretended she despised drugs, but on the way home she stopped at an automated teller machine and withdrew $40—enough for two $20 sticks of PCP. Then she partied with her friends.

Like many substance abusers, Kenya did not understand her drug use. Her explanations vary: She was getting back at her mother; drugs were dangerously exciting, plentiful, and cheap; she responded to peer pressure. Whatever the cause, Kenya descended from her secure, middle-class background into the netherworld of drugs.

In 1985, Kenya inhaled crack cocaine for the first time. Three months later, she was hooked on the cocaine high—far more potent than PCP, and far costlier. She started going to a rundown house in her neighborhood that reminded her of "The Twilight Zone," where people were doing crack day and night. There, an unemployed auto mechanic and small-time pusher named Delroy offered Kenya all the crack she wanted for free.

Delroy wasn't her type: He had no career goals and was handicapped by a drug-induced stroke, but over the next five years she accepted his professions of love in return for drugs. High on crack, Kenya found the environment an ideal life for a drug addict.

In 1988, she was working at Science Applications International Corporation, earning $2,000 a month, and sharing a condominium. A motherly supervisor learned of Kenya's drug habit and tried to cover for her. But her absences and erratic behavior were too frequent to hide; she was told to seek drug counseling. After she failed to comply, she was fired.

On the thin edge, strung out and cut off from her family, Kenya plunged into the abyss. Seeing no way out of her addiction, she decided to end her life on drugs once and for all. Alone in the condo, she emptied the medicine cabinet into her mouth, swallowing handfulls of Valium, Halcyon, codeine—more than 70 pills in all. She awoke in Paradise Valley Hospital, where doctors said they couldn't believe she had survived the overdose. Her parents came to the hospital, wanting to help her but not knowing how. She felt they were pretending her suicide attempt didn't happen.

The day after Kenya went home, she resumed crack to numb herself. She moved in with Delroy and stayed perpetually high. Early in 1989, her menstrual periods stopped. Pregnant with Delroy's child, she was too despondent to get help.

A responsible adult in full consciousness would have sought prenatal care and drug counseling, but people like Kenya who are heavily under the influence of drugs (and alcohol) are incapable of caring for themselves, much less others. Outreach programs are an effective way to provide drug counseling and prenatal care to women who do not seek it for themselves. Yet, in the middle of the drug-baby epidemic, America bowed to pressure from antiabortion groups and restricted access to reproductive services for poor women who needed it most. Over the past decade, more than 1,000 federal contraceptive clinics were forced to close, leaving roughly 5 million pregnant women at risk, according to Harriet Stinson, who started the country's first family-planning program for jail inmates.

Following the death of her son, Kenya struggled against drugs, with temporary attempts at sobriety. After a second suicide attempt at her parents' home in November 1989, she received treatment at the county mental health center. But the grossly overcrowded and underfunded facility had no beds available for long-term psychiatric care, and she was sent home after two days. She joined a twelve-step Narcotics Anonymous program and stayed clean long enough to go back to work as a word processor—ironically, for the county health department.

Staying clean became more difficult after Delroy was released from jail in March 1990. Delroy returned to dealing drugs and Kenya soon went back to her old haunts and habits. By summer, she was using crack daily; her life was unraveling, again. Desperately avoiding thoughts of suicide, she turned herself over to a detox program covered by county employees' health insurance.

As her head began to clear, she was mortified to discover she was pregnant by Delroy again.

Kenya wanted her baby to be healthy, but she didn't have the inner discipline to stay off crack for a week, let alone the eight remaining months of her pregnancy. A social worker told her that long-term treatment programs had waiting lists, but she might be able to enter an experimental treatment program especially designed for mothers.

Options for Recovery was located in San Marcos, far from the neighborhood that tempted Kenya with drugs. On her own initiative, Kenya called Options director Jean Comer. After hearing Kenya's history, there was no hesitation in Jean's voice: Kenya needed attention right away.

"How soon could you get here?" Jean asked.

Kenya's brother drove her up to Options that afternoon, August 1, 1990. She would always remember it as the date when her life changed and she began to come clean.

The intense middle-aged white woman who took Kenya in was a mother, drug therapist, and former stockbroker who also happened to be a recovered cocaine addict. Looking younger than her fifty-four years, short and sinewy, with riveting pale-blue eyes and cropped brown hair, Jean's tough, no-nonsense manner masked enormous reserves of warmth and compassion.

She believed that instead of sterilizing drug-abusing mothers or throwing them in prison (as many angry people advocated), these women should be given a choice to join a drug-free therapeutic community where they could gain a sense of self-worth and self-control—and deliver healthy babies. They came under a "velvet hammer," as Jean described the court orders for drug treatment required in order for mothers to regain babies placed in protective custody. Unlike most participants, Kenya entered Options by her own choice. Jean believed this personal commitment was a key to recovery.

At a time when Washington had all but given up on drug rehabilitation and was hurling billions into a losing War on Drugs, innovative efforts such as Options were among the nation's only positive responses to the people the rest of society had written off. An experimental program funded by San Diego County from state taxes on tobacco, Options has successfully engaged support from the local conservative community. It meets a desperate need in a pragmatic, no-frills manner, providing day-care treatment to mothers and babies, while running a small residence for a few mothers without homes.

The $250,000 grant that funded Options in 1989 specified that it must document what happened to each woman who enrolled in the program. If, after two years, Options couldn't show decisive results—clean mothers and clean babies—it would be terminated. For the thirty-two women in the program, some middle-class, some poor, the bottom-line rule was simple: Use drugs and you're kicked out. Every day, the mothers gave each other drug tests and the results were shown to the group. Since peer pressure had gotten many of the women into trouble with drugs in the first place, peer pressure was used to get them to stop and to keep them straight.

Options was housed in a cluster of warehouses on a highway frontage road between an office furniture outlet and an electronics depot. Pregnant mothers with heroin tracks on their arms or tattoos on their bodies wheeled baby carriages through the parking lot. They all looked out of place in the sterile business park, but within Options's doors was a "warm house," as Jean called it.

The 2,000-square-foot center, located in a separate wing of the warehouse complex, had its own entrance; it was painted bright colors and decorated with children's drawings. Counseling offices with windows to the parking lot surrounded a central meeting room that had no windows. In the back room, there was a day-care center for babies and toddlers. Options was a new, untested program on a low budget with no guarantee of success. For Kenya, it was her last hope.

After breaking down on August 19, Kenya went through three stages of withdrawal and healing at Options. She describes it like this: First, she was in a fog. Her body still had substances in it, but she was learning to break the habit. She needed close supervision, and every day was an agonizing struggle. Then her mind began to clear and her body began to feel clean for the first time, but she still did not trust herself to think that she could stay that way. Gradually, she began to take more responsibility for herself, but there were still moments of crisis when she needed help. Finally, after a couple of months she began to see herself clearly for the first time, and it seemed like a horrible dream that she had ever endangered her baby with drugs. She wanted to leave treatment totally independent, but this required preparation. She had to relearn how to live in the world. But she also worried about her ability to stay clean once she was back in the old neighborhood.

Not everything went smoothly between August and her projected delivery date in April. The cardinal rule against using drugs while enrolled at Options was eventually broken by a few of the women. While drunk, one mother tripped and nearly crushed a baby crawling on the floor. Kenya's own confidence to stay clean was threatened by the breakdown of discipline. Finally, after much agonizing, she decided to confront the drinkers in front of the group. One of the women, a friend, accused her of betraying their friendship. Kenya was stung, but instead of bowing to criticism, she chose to defend her own recovery. After a long debate, the group voted to put the women on a strict curfew but allowed them to remain in Options.

Such leniency increased the tensions building in this pressure cooker of a home run by Options, where several women and their babies shared the same bathroom and kitchen. Tempers rose to the flashing point, and Kenya blew up twice over seemingly insignificant disputes. In one incident, Kenya grabbed a butcher's knife and threatened to slit the throat of a woman who would not accede to Kenya's urgent requests to use the phone. The police came, but the woman didn't press charges. In a second incident, Kenya became convinced that Jean Comer had overcharged her because she was black. She rampaged into the director's office, threatening to kill Jean. Luckily, Jean had already gone for the day.

The rage in Kenya had little to do with these circumstances and more to do with the emotions that erupted from her past as she went through withdrawal from drugs and stripped herself bare. Kenya was told to leave the safe house, although the group voted to allow her to remain in Options. She moved into a small nearby apartment with another program member. Jean arranged for Kenya to receive individual psychological counseling, and she began confronting her childhood abuse and anger against her mother. Slowly, she began to separate from childhood helplessness, to find ways to emote without exploding, to depend on herself by relying on others.

The guiding principle of successful helping programs like Options is that reliance builds autonomy. Ironically, throughout her first pregnancy Kenya was self-reliant to the extreme, alienating herself from her family and society. Now, shielded by the therapeutic community of

Options for Recovery, Kenya was able to free herself from drugs and protect the child developing in her womb. She also received proper nutrition from a federal program called WIC, and prenatal care from Kaiser Permanente Hospital, where she was treated as a county employee on disability leave. Carefully, she nurtured her baby through the stages of prenatal development.

While Kenya was in treatment, efforts were being made in cities across America to cope with the crack-baby epidemic. In San Diego, prenatal care for high-risk women was being pioneered at The Birth Place, a low-cost birth center located near the university hospital where Kenya's first baby died. Among the first Medicaid-funded birth centers in America, The Birth Place provides a comprehensive program of prenatal care and delivery for mothers turned away by private doctors. Nurse midwives supervised by medical-school physicians deliver babies for nearly half the cost of a private doctor. Low-income patients are treated with dignity in a quiet, family-oriented environment that resembles a bed and breakfast more than a hospital. If an emergency develops, however, the patient is rushed to the nearby university hospital.

Every dollar spent on prenatal care saves three dollars in emergency care, and as much as seven dollars in long-term care, according to national studies. The Birth Place is proof that America can provide excellent, cost-effective prenatal care to poor, uninsured women who need it most.

When it came time for Kenya to deliver, she went to Kaiser Permanente, which provided comprehensive prenatal care and delivery for employees enrolled in its health maintenance organization (HMO). There, accompanied by her mother, everything about her second delivery—down to the expressions on the faces of the nurses—seemed more hopeful and positive. With the drugs out of her body, she was fully conscious and clear. This time she was excited, hoping for a girl. It was a stark contrast with her first delivery. When the new child was born by cesarean section on March 28, 1991, she felt that she was being reborn as a person. Her heart was filled with joy when they placed a healthy boy in her arms. She named him Miles.

Kenya brought Miles from the hospital to her parents' home, where they were given a special room. The recovering mother and her baby were welcomed by Kenya's parents, who agreed to provide a place for her to live as long as she remained clean. Kenya received $560 a month in Aid to Families with Dependent Children (AFDC), about one third of her former salary, and gave $100 a month to her parents to help defray expenses. Her goal was to stay home with her baby for six months before going back to college and studying computer science.

Eight months after I heard Kenya cry out in drug treatment, I visited her and two-week-old Miles at her parents' home in Southeast San Diego. The big, long-limbed baby was asleep, his cheeks round as moons under the crescents of his closed eyes. Kenya looked calmer and more grounded; she seemed to have lost her angry bitterness, as if becoming a mother had given her a new perspective. While I was there, Jean Comer stopped by to see how they were doing.

"Another clean baby!" Jean crowed, sweeping up Miles in her arms. "Kenya is interrupting the chain. When you see a clean baby born, that shows the chance for real change." Jean took a breath, her enthusiasm gushing out, leaving her deflated.

"My mom is very ill," Jean said, suddenly. She

explained that she had left Options to take care of her mother, who suffered from emphysema. "Believe me, it's a lot harder to take care of your own."

Options for Recovery, proven effective beyond Jean's dreams, is continuing under another director because Jean had to take care of her own mother. In its first two years, twenty-four babies were born; not one of them tested positive for drugs. These results convinced California's Medicaid agency, MediCal, to pay for Options treatments on an ongoing basis, giving the go-ahead for the program to continue beyond its two-year experimental stage.

This makes dollar sense: The cost of Options's treatment is $60 per day, compared to $2,000 a day for a baby in neonatal intensive care. The program's survival in the near term seemed assured, but because of fluctuating state budgets, the life span of even highly successful programs is often tragically short. I wonder if Options will endure to help others survive.

Our voices awakened Miles, who opened his dark-brown eyes and looked up at the adults cooing and hovering over him. He may never know the role Jean played in his life, nor what his mother overcame to bear him. But it should be acknowledged that this little boy owes his life to a model program, created in one community, that can be adapted to fit the needs of other communities.

Proudly, Kenya held her baby. Jean stood by her. Kenya's father, arriving home from work, joined his daughter and grandson to have the moment recorded in a snapshot.

"I believe this is what the new family looks like," said Jean. "Me as a sort of surrogate mother-sister. Here's a new-style, old-style grandfather." She smiled at a little girl, Delroy's daughter, who was visiting her baby half-brother. "We're learning new ways to be together."

"All these people were part of my recovery," Kenya

said, gesturing around the circle. The baby lay at the center: strong, healthy, and beloved.

Cindy Miller's baby, Nicholas, was also blessed with good health and the attentions of a loving family. But Cindy ran the risk of blood clots if she became pregnant again. Although the swelling in her leg disappeared after Nicholas's birth, Dr. Lyons forbade her to take birth-control pills because they sometimes caused clotting. When, by chance, she conceived again, a year and a half later, he cautioned Cindy that phlebitis might recur. Two months into her second pregnancy, Cindy experienced severe pain in her left leg. Once more, she was back in the hospital, and back on heparin to dissolve the blood clot that had already formed.

This time Cindy was presented with a horrifying set of choices: If she terminated this pregnancy, she could never take the risk of getting pregnant again; if she went through with it, either she or the baby, or both of them, could die. If her body responded to heparin for a long-enough period—seven months—she could expect to deliver a healthy child. But if her body started rejecting the drug, there could be serious problems: New blood clots could form, or she could be forced to use other medications that would threaten the baby.

Her parents wanted her to terminate the pregnancy. But Cindy refused even to consider an abortion. She thought it selfish to sacrifice a child's life because of some physical inconvenience. As an only child of divorced parents, her deepest desire was to have a large brood of children raising the roof with their shouts and laughter. Cindy and Tim considered life precious from the moment of conception, and they were willing to take any risk to give Nicholas the gift of a little sister or brother. As far as the financial risks of a sick child, they felt secure (and grateful) for Cindy's hospital-employee health insurance policy and certain that they could meet any peripheral expenses. Since Dr. Lyons told Cindy that very premature baby girls have a better chance of making it than do premature boys, Cindy prayed for a girl.

Working part-time at the hospital, wearing an IV in her hand, taking every precaution, she had a miserable pregnancy. Because severe morning sickness and daylong nausea kept her from being able to eat much, Cindy gained only five pounds in five months.

Her body started to resist the heparin. One day she began to hemorrhage. Dr. Lyons advised her to get bed rest and stay off her feet. But when the cramping began, she realized she was in labor. By Sunday night, he admitted her to the hospital and gave her an injection to stop the contractions. Tim was away on business in Cincinnati, and couldn't get back for several hours. Cindy would be alone and in labor all night, with fetal monitors checking the heartbeat of her baby.

"You don't have a stomach to monitor this," the nurse said, indicating her patient's small belly. Cindy prayed her labor pains would stop and watched her baby's heart waves on the fetal monitor. She whispered to the child heaving in her belly, trying to calm the baby down. Cindy received two more injections of anticontraction drugs, but they didn't work. By Monday morning, the worst thing possible happened: Her water broke. She now had twenty-four hours to deliver a baby who was nearly four months premature.

When Tim, who'd driven all night, arrived at Cindy's room that morning, he found it jammed with six or seven nurses frantically rushing around her bed. He panicked, afraid a blood clot had gone to her heart. Instead, his wife was in heavy labor. Since the community hospital in

Wabash was ill-equipped to treat a baby who was four months premature, they decided to transfer her to a regional hospital in Fort Wayne, fifty miles away. While they loaded Cindy into the ambulance, Tim, who hadn't slept in two days, took off in his van. The ambulance passed him doing eighty-five miles an hour.

At Parkview Hospital, they rolled Cindy into a delivery room. Dr. William Lewis, a neonatologist, waited on alert with an obstetrician, Dr. William Graham. Dr. Graham took ultrasound measure of what was going on inside her womb: The baby was coming in breach. He informed Cindy bluntly that her baby had less than a 30 percent chance of surviving, then said as gently as he could, "If I take you into surgery now, you'll bleed to death because of the heparin. If I give you blood thickener, you could throw a clot that will probably kill both of you."

Out in the hall, the obstetrician told Tim he might have to choose whether to save the baby or save his wife—but he was determined to save both. Tim said to save Cindy first; the doctor waited as long as possible for the residue of heparin to pass from her body and her blood to thicken before operating. Contractions grew more intense and frequent, but Cindy managed to extend labor another eight hours. At midnight Tuesday, they took her into the cold surgical delivery room. Before going under the anesthetic, Cindy pleaded with Dr. Graham to do everything he could to save her baby.

When she came to, she heard a nurse's voice and immediately asked groggily about the baby.

"You had a boy. He only weighs one pound thirteen ounces," the nurse answered. Knowing the terrible odds for Cindy's child, the nurse added, deliberately, "He's as stable as he can be."

Cindy refused to be taken back to her room before seeing her newborn son. They wheeled her from the recovery room into the neonatal intensive-care unit; it was frighteningly silent. She saw isolettes that held no-care babies, crack-exposed infants, babies with HIV, and low-birthweight babies such as the Millers' son, fighting one by one for their lives.

They drew Cindy beside an incubator covered with tinfoil. Through a porthole, she saw a tiny, crimson body. Wrenched from the fetal position, he lay on his stomach, with his legs splayed. A needle was stuck in his cribbed hand. His back, no longer than her baby finger, was covered with monitors and heaved up and down. His bald head was covered by a minuscule pink ski cap. "Why is my son wearing a pink cap?" she demanded, strangely offended. A nurse muttered an apology and said she'd be sure to get a boy's blue cap.

Cindy's son was so small, she could have covered him with her hand. She reached out but could not touch him through the glass. He lay in the center of a tiny sheepskin the size of typing paper, resting on a "waterbed" made from a fluid bag. His eyes were covered with a mask to reduce jaundice. His skin was so transparent, she could see every single vein. Though he looked as though he were crying, he made no sound, for his trachea had been cut and a breathing tube inserted. His severely undeveloped lungs gasped for oxygen through a ventilator. She looked up at the other babies and their parents, each with a story, and she realized that the silent screams of these babies were unheard by the outside world.

The two-day labor had utterly drained Cindy, but fortunately, and unbeknownst to her, it had pushed forward development of the baby's lungs by a crucial phase, saving his life. When the orderly finally took Cindy to her hospital room, she fell asleep instantly. When she awoke later and called downstairs to the nursery to ask about her son, she was told he had lost eight precious ounces since birth, now weighing little more than one pound. She told the nurse she wanted to thank them all and to tell them her son's name. "It's Andrew James Miller," she said proudly, never doubting he would survive, but unaware of the impending financial crisis that would come from his hospitalization. "We're going to call him A.J."

A.J. Miller was born on August 1, 1989, the same month and year that Kenya Williams's firstborn died. In a twist of fate, Kenya's strapping new baby, Miles Karim Williams, weighed five times as much as A.J. at birth. The cost of A.J.'s hospitalization would pay for drug treatment for all the women enrolled in Options during the two-year experiment—nearly sixty mothers.

INFANCY

A.J.

America's progress in reducing infant mortality is written in baby footprints that are getting progressively smaller and fainter. At the beginning of the twentieth century, it was commonplace for families to suffer the loss of a baby. Decade by decade, advances in public health and private medicine slowly reduced the toll of infant mortality. After World War II, the United States became a world leader in neonatal care. With the War on Poverty in the mid 1960s, infant mortality among the poor began to decline rapidly. But by the late 1980s, cuts in public health programs, soaring medical costs, and the drug-baby epidemic slowed progress to a snail's pace. In 1992, America slipped to twenty-second place in infant mortality, the highest rate among its Western allies.*

Infant mortality is a critical measure of a nation's health—and prognosis for its children's future. "Our survival as a human community may depend as much upon our nurture of love in infancy and childhood as upon the protection of our society from external threats," wrote Selma Fraiberg, an expert in child development.

---

* Americans whose forebears immigrated from Australia, Austria, Belgium, Canada, Denmark, Finland, France, Germany, Greece, Hong Kong, Ireland, Italy, Japan, the Netherlands, Norway, Singapore, Spain, Sweden, Switzerland, and the United Kingdom will be startled to learn that babies born in their countries of origin now have a higher rate of survival than babies in the United States. The U.S. mortality rate of 9.8 per 1,000 live births is more than double that of our foremost economic competitor, Japan (4.59).

Babies' survival is jeopardized by contradictory impulses in American society to spend limitlessly to save some babies while neglecting the basic needs of others. At the low end of the scale, babies fail to thrive because of lack of health care, poor nutrition, physical abuse, and neglect. At the high end, premature babies are saved by high-tech miracles costing hundreds of thousands of dollars. Rich or poor, low-birthweight babies (below 2,500 grams or 5.5 pounds) share one thing in common: Their chance of dying in the first month of life is forty times greater than that of normal-weight babies.

A.J. was born at the cusp of fetal viability—so premature that he could have been aborted. His footprints at birth were one-third the size of his brother Nicholas's footprints—so small that, if he could have walked, A.J. could have taken four steps across this page. His chances of surviving were only fifty-fifty.

A premature baby's struggle for life involves five basic processes: First, a baby has seven or eight minutes to breathe before the brain is gone. Oxygen, which entered through the placenta, must now come from the lungs. Second, a baby has to maintain temperature: Small babies get cold fast and must be put in an incubator to stay warm. Third, an infant must mobilize food from internal stores within minutes, or have low blood sugar and get in trouble. Fourth, the kidneys have to start working to get rid of waste products. Fifth, the intestines must absorb food, and the bowels pump it out.

"All of these processes must take place at once," says Dr. Lewis, A.J.'s neonatologist. "If they don't all happen, whammo, you're dead."

A.J. needed assistance for all five processes. He didn't breathe. He was put on a ventilator, a blue box with dials that forced air in and out of his lungs sixty times a minute. He was hooked up to eight monitors. He had a tube in his belly button and patches on his chest to monitor heart rate. He was put in a warmer resembling a broiler, and then into an isolette, similar to a hot room. A probe constantly measured his body temperature. A tube down his nose kept his stomach from blowing up. When he got upset, he'd make crying motions. Air in his stomach gave him trouble breathing. Doctors had to maintain adequate sugar and give A.J. suppositories to make him evacuate and provide nutrition via a vein.

A.J. clung to a sheepskin in an artificial womb, struggling for life with each breath. Unable to feel his mother's heartbeat or suckle her breast, he breathed oxygenated air while his heart circulated donated blood. He was defenseless, utterly dependent on a mechanical world that attempted to replicate the functions of the human body.

The inner world of an infant in intensive care is not reassuring. Pain is predictable and human touch infrequent. When A.J.'s heartbeat slowed, he was startled awake by alarms that stimulated it. The sharp prick of a needle made his fists clench, his face contort, and his mouth wrench open.

A.J. screamed soundlessly and saw darkness patched with eerie blue light. A ventilator breathed for him, bypassing his vocal cords, and a new baby-blue boy's hat was pulled over his eyes to block out the warming lights. When the noises died away, he heard the beating of a simulated heart pinned to the sheet, and the murmur of his mother's voice playing on a portable tape recorder. He smelled sheepskin and felt water sloshing below him. Sometimes a hand would reach through a porthole and try to touch and comfort him. Once, he pushed against the incubator door.

"He's trying to get out!" the nurse joked. Cindy laughed, and A.J. turned his head toward his mother.

Almost from birth, he seemed to know her voice. She reached out, unable to cradle her son in the isolette. He was so vulnerable, but he had a fighting spirit.

After six days, Cindy was discharged from the hospital, but A.J. remained under the care of his personal nurse, Peggy Jagodzinski. Going home to a house filled with sympathy cards—many relatives doubted A.J. would survive—provoked the emptiest feeling in the world. As long as A.J. had been inside her, she felt he was safe. But now her body was stitched and stapled together, and in the center she felt an emptiness.

The day after Cindy left, A.J.'s lung collapsed from pneumonia. Cindy rushed up from Wabash; the doctor pumped up his lung and A.J. survived.

"I thought A.J. was dead three times," Dr. Lewis recalls. "He was a very tenuous kid, always on the brink of checking out."

Cindy hovered over her son, respectfully assisting doctors and nurses. Scrubbed and gowned, she reached through a porthole, sponging his skin, wiping his lips, feeding him milk pumped from her breast—all in the hope A.J. would know his mother.

Seventeen days passed before Cindy could hold her son. They wrapped A.J. in a blanket and ran his ventilator tube through Cindy's blouse so he could continue breathing as she held him. She cradled A.J. under huge heat lamps and cried, feeling her son tethered to tubes in a blanket.

A.J. had sixteen transfusions the first month. When they ran out of veins to draw blood, they imbedded an intravenous tube in the soft spot at the top of his head.

Premature infants are only capable of learning one skill at a time. When A.J. was taken off the respirator to breathe air for the first time, his bowels stopped functioning. Every time A.J. tried to cry, Cindy cried for him.

She was afraid that her son Nicholas would feel excluded, so she frequently took him to visit his baby brother. "Hi, A.J.," the nineteen-month-old would say, plopping down beside the incubator to play with stuffed animals.

When A.J. reached three pounds, Cindy celebrated the milestone by throwing a party for the staff. A.J. wore clothes from a Cabbage Patch doll that were still too big for him.

Cindy was allowed a total of eight weeks' maternity leave from her job. A.J. was still in the hospital in Fort Wayne when she went back to work at the hospital in Wabash, where she was responsible for marketing, advertising, and public relations. It was a tremendous strain to work for eight hours and commute between A.J.'s bedside and home.

The emotional, financial, and time pressures on families like the Millers are tremendous; not surprisingly, 80 percent of marriages with very sick babies fail. Working parents with sick children need to take family leave. President Bush vetoed family leave bills that would have helped the Millers, but President Clinton signed family leave legislation into law soon after taking office. Although the 1993 family leave law excludes small businesses with few employees, such as Tim's carpet-laying company, the hospital where Cindy worked will now be compelled to provide family leave to mothers with sick babies—too late for A.J.

America still lags behind our European and Japanese allies in providing comprehensive health services to pregnant women and families with young children. Most developed countries consider newborns a benefit to society and help parents cope with the added burden.

France pays pregnant women $34 a month to get prenatal checkups; 99 percent comply, reducing the number of low-birthweight babies. Paid maternity leave is common in Western European countries, some for periods up to two years. Sweden, Germany, Spain, and Belgium pay a one-time cash benefit to parents of newborns, while other countries pay a supplement ranging from 5 to 10 percent of wages. They also provide free or subsidized health care to all children.

Increasingly, poverty in America means not only lack of money, but lack of access to health care. In Dr. Lewis's ward, for example, one-fourth of the babies received little or no prenatal care; a third had no health insurance and no ability to pay. One baby ran up a $650,000 bill, but because of a dispute over the mother's residence, Medicaid reimbursed the hospital only $3,550.

"You have to cry," says Dr. Lewis, reflecting on hundreds of babies he has watched die unnecessarily. "If you don't, you can't take care of the next baby. I feel rotten about our system. You spend eighteen to twenty hours over two days fighting like hell to solve a problem that could have been solved in ten minutes with good prenatal care. You see a baby dying or brain-damaged, despite your work, and know that with a little bit of education or help, this could have been prevented. It makes you sick. You want to pound on someone's head. You don't know who to pound on. You're making a dent in a wall that's solid steel."

Dr. Lewis was especially angered by parents who refused to take advantage of prenatal care and drug treatment. But the Millers were different. "Cindy is a rather unforgettable person," Dr. Lewis reflects. "We don't have many mothers who are as assertive—and friendly—as she is. Cindy is one of those people who would listen to you, thank you, and always ask challenging questions: 'What can we do? What are the options and alternatives?' Most people are very reliant on physicians to guide them along, in order not to make decisions. The Millers always wanted to know, to participate in A.J.'s care and make the decisions."

A.J. remained in the hospital for three and a half months, the time he normally would have gestated in the womb. Even after his discharge, he was at risk for sudden infant death syndrome (SIDS), and needed a device called an apnea monitor that would ring an alarm when he stopped breathing. A nurse warned Cindy of a mother who unplugged the apnea monitor and fell asleep with her baby suckling her breast; she awoke with a dead child in her arms.

A.J. came home on a cold day of autumn storms. A truck from the medical equipment company followed after, bearing a liquid oxygen tank. Friends had tied blue and white balloons around the yard. Cindy insisted that A.J.'s bedroom feel like a child's nursery, not a hospital room, so the tank was put in the living room, where it would remain for two years, and tubes ran under the carpet to A.J.'s room. Tim had an oak cradle specially made for A.J. Cindy placed her son on a tiny sheepskin in the cradle. After three and a half months, he only weighed four pounds. Oblivious to his homecoming, he went right to sleep.

The first apnea alarm went off that afternoon. Cindy jostled A.J. awake and he resumed breathing, a pattern that went on night after night. A.J. had a rigorous schedule that demanded round-the-clock attention. He had to eat every three hours and receive a breathing treatment every four hours. In order to get some sleep between feedings and work, Cindy arranged for a home nurse to stay from midnight to 8 A.M.

Two weeks later, one of the nurses came in sick. Preemies have virtually no defenses, and within hours, A.J. came down with a savage cold; he couldn't breathe

39

and started turning blue. In the middle of the night, the Millers bundled him up with an oxygen tank and drove him to Fort Wayne, where the Parkview staff were waiting with life-support equipment. Cindy sat in a hard, wooden chair beside A.J.'s bed and prayed that if he survived, she would be better prepared for his next home emergency.

But no one prepared her for the cumulative cost of medical care. A.J. stayed for two weeks in the pediatric intensive care unit; the bill for his second hospital stay was $25,000. Cindy watched his medical bills mounting and began to fear that his health insurance wouldn't last the winter. The first indication something was drastically wrong with A.J.'s coverage came when the hospital social worker made a routine call to the insurance company to find out if home nursing was covered by the family's policy.

The insurance company informed her that A.J.'s total lifetime health coverage was $250,000. At the time of his initial discharge, A.J.'s hospital bill was $189,000. After the second bill was added, only $36,000 of benefits remained *for his entire life*. Worse, Cindy learned that because of A.J.'s "preexisting condition," no insurer would sell additional insurance that they could even begin to afford. The social worker advised Cindy to apply for help from a fund for crippled children and try to get A.J. on Medicaid, but because they were employed, she doubted the latter would be possible.

The Millers, like millions of working Americans with serious health problems in the family, faced a crisis they never expected. The prevailing belief in the United States is that private medicine and health insurance are superior to government medical care and insurance. But the "magic of the marketplace" failed to provide affordable private health insurance to babies like A.J. While 37 million Americans went without any health insurance, government cutbacks imposed restrictions on health care for the poor, known as Medicaid.

The Millers were not poor, but solidly middle-class. Neither Cindy nor Tim had ever asked for public assistance, but had supported themselves by working hard since they were teenagers. As they brought A.J. home from the hospital for the second time, fear lodged in their throats. Not only was A.J. vulnerable to every cold, but they faced expending his remaining insurance. How could they pay the bills? Three and a half months of hospitalization had cost more than their total combined income for six years. Home nursing and equipment was costing an additional $8,000 a month—double their take-home earnings. What if their insurance ran out and A.J. needed to be hospitalized again? Cindy had heard of poor people being dumped from hospitals, but she had never identified with them before; the "homeless" were somehow different, and the Millers owned their own home. Cindy shivered in the car, computing how long it would take after A.J.'s insurance ran out before they stopped paying their mortgage and lost their home.

As their sense of security crumbled, Cindy and Tim pledged that somehow they would make it. The important thing was that A.J. was alive. Cindy had faith in the system she had supported as a campaign worker for Dan Quayle's Senate campaign. She truly believed that in America no child would be turned away from medical care and no working family would be forced into poverty because of a sick baby.

In order to apply for Medicaid, Cindy discovered that she would have to go through the local welfare office, which sounded strange to a college-educated, professional working woman. She swallowed her pride and called for an appointment, but the phones were always busy. Finally,

she reached someone in the governor's office and complained about the delays. That day, a welfare caseworker
called her back and made a 4 P.M. appointment. Cindy
reached the office ten minutes ahead of time. She sat
down on a hard, wooden bench and looked around her.
The room was dismal and she felt humiliated.

At 4:25, a white-haired man with a large birthmark on
his hand walked up and asked coldly if she were Mrs.
Miller. He looked her up and down. She felt self-conscious
even though she wore a pair of nice blue jeans and a
blouse, and her hair was clean.

Cindy's feeling of guilt came as a shock to her. She had
always paid taxes and believed that services were available for those in need. Like many taxpayers, she was concerned about government waste and inefficiency, and she
was outraged by President Reagan's stories of welfare
fraud, but she never thought a mother like herself would
be silently accused of asking for something she didn't
need or deserve. And what's more, she was responsible
for A.J., a child who couldn't come down here and defend
himself. She felt suddenly naked and powerless before a
low-level government official standing over her. The caseworker raked her with his critical glance and walked
away. She followed him down a long, narrow corridor and
later gave this account of their meeting:

"This will be a short appointment," he began coldly.
"Our office closes at four-thirty and we don't stay over."
He looked at her cynically. "Frankly, we don't get paid
enough to care."

She sat up in her chair and said, "Sir, I think you're in
the wrong profession."

"The way I see it, you basically have three alternatives," he said, not mincing words. "One, get a divorce,
and welfare will pick up Medicaid. Two, spend down to

the poverty level." *Spending down* was a euphemism for exhausting all one's financial resources before qualifying for assistance. Cindy and Tim would have to sell their house and cars and expend their savings. "Three, give the child up to the state. Put him in a nursing home or an institution."

There was absolutely no way that she was going to give A.J. up to the state, and the suggestion of divorce was equally outrageous.

The caseworker stared at her impassively. "Would you be willing to sell your home?" he asked.

"No."

"You mean to tell me," he insisted angrily, "you wouldn't be willing to sell a house to help your child?"

"Let's get something straight right now," Cindy answered. "I would do anything for my child. But I can't see selling our home and causing turmoil for our older son and moving to an apartment where you pay the same rent as we already pay in house payments. What is that proving?"

He just stared at her. "You're both working. What about all these people who don't have jobs? They need help more than you do."

"I'm not asking for welfare or food stamps. All I'm asking for is medical help for my baby."

She had brought A.J.'s medical discharge, to show he was medically eligible for Medicaid, as well as their tax returns, savings passbook, and mortgage receipts. They were proud to have paid a little extra each month on their mortgage to bring down the $49,000 principal they had borrowed on their $55,000 house. Would this now be to their credit, or used against them?

The caseworker praised her thoroughness, but asked her to provide a complete list of their possessions.

"Do you have a safety deposit box?"

"Yes."

"You are required to open it in the presence of a bank officer, who must list all its contents."

She suspected that because they were middle-class, the caseworker assumed they were taking the system for a ride. She explained they had astronomical medical bills, but he didn't seem to take them into account.

"It will be six to seven months for an answer on Medicaid."

Cutting short the interview, he walked her out to her car. At first, she thought he felt bad and was trying to be polite. But then he wrote down the make and model of her car and, leaning inside, took down the serial number.

"What are you doing?" Cindy asked. They had bought the used 1986 Chrysler LeBaron GTS after attending a kickoff rally in Huntington, Indiana, for Dan Quayle in the 1988 presidential campaign. Now she wondered if the U.S. government was going to take it away from her.

"With two vehicles, it goes against you," he said. "You're a Christian, aren't you?"

"Yes."

He smiled coldly, "I'll pray for you."

She started home with no hope of getting any assistance. Even though A.J. was medically eligible, the Millers were not financially eligible for Medicaid in Indiana. The Medicaid program is mandated by the federal government, but each state pays a share of costs and is free to determine its own eligibility standards. Indiana was then one of twelve states where applicants were, euphemistically speaking, "allowed to spend down" (actually forced to become paupers) before receiving Medicaid. In thirty-one states and the District of Columbia, babies who are deemed disabled are automatically eligible for Medicaid. Eight states have other formulas for granting aid.*

After this visit to the welfare office, Cindy sat down and wrote a letter to Vice-President Quayle.

December 29, 1989

Dear Mr. Vice-President,

My name is Cindy Miller. Several years ago I campaigned for you when you ran against Bayh for Senate, under my maiden name DuBuque. I supported you and we won, and now I desperately need your support.

My husband and I have two small sons. The oldest will be two in January and the youngest was born August 1, 1989, fifteen weeks premature. . . . He spent the first three and a half months of his life in Parkview's neonatal intensive care unit, much of the time on a ventilator and oxygen. While the ventilator kept him alive, it also caused damage to his lungs, known as Hyline Membrane Disease.

Since my husband is independently employed as a carpet layer, I carry medical insurance on the entire family. . . . When our son was first born, I checked into the insurance and they said we were fine and that the most we would have to pay would be $100

---

* The twelve states with the most restrictive criteria for Medicaid eligibility are: Connecticut, Hawaii, Illinois, Indiana, Minnesota, Missouri, New Hampshire, North Carolina, North Dakota, Ohio, Oklahoma, and Virginia. These states fall into a category known as 209(b). According to the House Ways and Means Committee's official *Green Book,* "aged, blind, and disabled Medicaid applicants must be allowed to spend down in 209(b) states." Cindy Miller says this is nonsense; she wasn't "allowed" to spend down to poverty, but forced to do so.

To prevent such horrors, the federal government should eliminate the 209(b) option and require all states to provide Medicaid to families such as the Millers.

deductible and $500 out of pocket. Right before we brought my son home on November 15, we checked to see if the insurance would pick up the equipment rental and the nursing ordered by the doctor at night so we could sleep. We were floored to find out that the hospital bill for our baby alone was up to $189,000 and that there is a $250,000 LIFETIME MAXIMUM per person. . . .

Our insurance is on the brink of maxing out now. There is absolutely no way to afford the premiums if we were to take out an insurance policy on him because of a preexisting condition. I'm not getting very far with Crippled Children's or Medicaid—they tell me that it could be seven months before we even have an answer!

My husband and I are honest, hardworking people. We have never asked for or taken any governmental funding. We've always worked and paid our own way. I'm not asking for welfare or food stamps now, only for medical help for my son. Put yourself in our place, Dan. How would you feel if it were your child and you kept getting the door slammed in your face? I've always believed in the system, but right now I have some serious doubts. Why is everything set up to benefit the very rich or the very poor with the middle-class people bearing the weight of it all?

We are not the only people in this situation. . . . Did you know that 10 percent of all the babies born in the United States today are premature? Seven of the ten require extended hospital stays and extended medical treatment at home. Who pays? If my husband and I didn't work and sat at home on our butts we wouldn't have a problem. Everything would be paid for! A serious indication that something is wrong with the system, don't you think?

My husband and I just turned 30 and we bought our first home three years ago. It's nothing fancy but we've put a lot of love into it, and it's the only home my boys have ever known. I don't want to lose it over medical bills. People are filing bankruptcies every day in our situation. We would only file as an absolute last resource [sic]. Who wins in a bankruptcy? Can anything be done? . . .

No one has an answer. Please Dan, won't you help us find the funding for our son? He's a perfect little baby who's just having to work a little harder to replace scar tissue around his lungs. Hopefully this will last less than a year and he'll be as good as new, with no permanent damage of any kind. I really feel that with all the brick walls we keep hitting, his rights are being violated. Where do I go from here? . . .

A mother from Ohio called me a couple of weeks ago. She was in a similar situation only with twins and was told in order to receive Medicaid she and her husband would have to get a divorce! The really sad thing is that they actually CONSIDERED it! If you or your staff could get involved, I know you could make a difference.

Our son will be five months old on New Year's Day and weighs just seven pounds. I want both him and his brother to grow up believing in our system . . . that one voice can be heard, one person can make a difference . . .

Sincerely,
Cindy A. Miller

Within three days of receiving her letter, Quayle's office jumped into action. Messages were dispatched to Indiana senator Dan Coats to investigate what was going on, and the vice-president himself reportedly told his staff to do everything possible, within the rules, to help the Millers. But getting them eligible for Medicaid in Indiana was not simple. The Millers would have to apply for an individual waiver from Medicaid rules. If this failed, they would have to lobby to change Indiana law, which, a senatorial aide told Cindy, would be nearly impossible. This only made her more committed to fight for A.J.

Her first objective was to get a waiver for her son. But Cindy didn't intend to stop there. She wanted to prevent other Indiana families from being pauperized just to get medical care. Vice-President Quayle's office gave the Millers the names and numbers of key political figures to contact in Indiana, but Cindy had to carry the ball herself. She contacted State Senator Harold "Podge" Wheeler, who was sympathetic to her cause. He later agreed to draft legislation, known as Senate Bill 30, making Medicaid eligibility based on medical need, not the financial status of a child's parents.

A few days later, Cindy got a call from the caseworker.

"I am not impressed," he said.

"Excuse me?"

"I'm not impressed that the White House called," he said. "So-and-so may be intimidated by Quayle's office. But I'm not."

Fearing reprisals, Cindy went to the newspapers with her story. The Wabash *Plain Dealer,* the Marion *Chronicle-Tribune,* and other newspapers came out with detailed accounts of the Miller's plight. Readers called Cindy to express their support. People in Wabash were shocked that a family would have to be broken up or bankrupted to get medical assistance for a child. Friends in the community began organizing a fund-raiser for the Millers.

On February 22, the First United Methodist Church

and Wabash County Hospital co-hosted a benefit at the 4-H Fair building to help pay the Millers' mounting medical debts. As luck would have it, the tenderloin dinner and silent auction took place on the stormiest night of the winter, with snow drifting high and the roads barely passable. In four-wheel-drive vehicles, hundreds of people trekked to the stark pole barn that lit up with the spirit of a community helping its own.

The benefit was an ordeal for the Millers, who didn't want to admit they needed help, but who deeply appreciated the generosity of their neighbors. An elderly couple told Cindy they had lost their grandchild because of the law restricting Medicaid, and they were contributing so that never again would an Indiana baby be denied medical care.

On a table were displayed Dan Quayle's cuff links and other donations for the silent auction. The community reached deep into its pockets, and the long line waiting for tenderloins overwhelmed the 4-H kitchen. When all was over, the fund-raiser collected $15,000—enough for a week in the hospital, or two months of home nursing. This was put into a fund for A.J., to be administered by the church.

After the event, things began to settle back to normal, if the Millers' exhausting schedule could be called that. Tim would start work before dawn and finish up at 4 P.M., just in time to pass Cindy running out the door to begin work at the hospital. She got off at 11 or 12 at night, then would rush home to A.J. When they could no longer afford nurses, Cindy would take the midnight-to-3-A.M. shift to watch over A.J., and Tim would then wake up and baby-sit him before heading out to lay carpet. For months, the Millers existed on two or three hours of sleep a night. They never went out together and always ate at home, saving every dime to keep themselves afloat.

A.J.'s insurance capped out in February. The fundraiser helped the Millers stay afloat for several months, but unpaid medical bills mounted to $60,000. Then bad news came. A personal waiver for A.J. was rejected. With bankruptcy imminent, Cindy saw no choice but to campaign to change the eligibility standards for all Indiana children.

Physically exhausted, but burning with passion for a cause that she now saw as greater than her son's plight, Cindy mounted a statewide lobbying campaign for Senate Bill 30. She called every legislator personally and told A.J.'s story to anyone who would listen. On A.J.'s first birthday, State Senator Wheeler invited her to Indianapolis to testify in a legislative hearing on behalf of his bill. Cindy felt terrible leaving A.J. with a baby-sitter on his first birthday, but she hoped the Legislature would end up giving him a more lasting gift.

Facing key legislators in the committee room packed with parents of other children in her situation, Cindy said: "Today as we celebrate our son's first birthday and we look back over the last twelve months, we are so grateful . . . grateful for the very fact that we have him and that once he outgrows his lung problems, he will be a totally perfect little boy; and grateful for the support of many caring people along the way. We are asking the State of Indiana to amend the state Medicaid plan. . . . While our main reason for being here today is A.J.," she concluded, "we are committed to finding an answer for all families in our situation. Our children are the future of this country, and even the very smallest deserve every opportunity."

Lobbying for her cause taught Cindy how the political

process worked. Beneath the ideology and the rhetoric, she discovered that politics came down to give-and-take, a glorified system of horse trades. The "system" was not set up to help people; rather, it seemed to hold you in the same place—or to make it worse.

Through the summer and into the second fall of A.J.'s life, Cindy continued to petition, to lobby, to campaign, and to call attention to the situation. The longer she struggled, the more she saw the inequities built into the system that foiled people's efforts to help themselves. She saw how other working families with huge medical bills were broken up or forced to "spend down to poverty," as the welfare bureaucrat had said, in order to be eligible for health care for their children.

At the end of the legislative session, Senate Bill 30 was held hostage to a political fight over redistricting. In the final hours before adjournment, Cindy made calls to key members. "You're playing with a human life," she pleaded. "This is not a piece of paper." At a few minutes before midnight on the final day of the session, April 30, 1991, the bill passed the Indiana Senate. A courier ran it down to the Indiana House of Representatives just in time to be voted on, passed, and signed into law.

May 1 was Cindy and Tim's eighth wedding anniversary. They went to a local restaurant and celebrated the passage of a state bill that would allow their family to remain together, knowing A.J. would be covered by Medicaid.

This law has helped many people in Indiana, especially people who think they have good insurance until they one day face catastrophic problems and have to impoverish themselves. America helps the poor, because the rich don't need it. But the working people are the ones who get hurt. Today, children like A.J., who pass stringent medical eligibility requirements, receive Medicaid without forcing their families into poverty in the Hoosier State.

Still, a dozen other states require families to become paupers to get Medicaid; horror stories abound. In Tennessee, a legal aid attorney describes the case of a mother whose frail newborn had trouble breathing and was provided with an apnea monitor covered by insurance. One day, a "repo man" appeared at the door and asked for the monitor back. The mother pleaded that the baby still needed it and explained that the doctor ordered it. But the man replied that he had written orders—the insurance had run out—and he removed the apnea monitor. The mother watched over her baby for as long as she could. But one night, overcome with exhaustion, she fell asleep. When she awoke, the baby was still and cold—dead. The attorney later discovered the doctor had made a clerical error in filling out the insurance form for the apnea monitor.

The cost of insuring catastrophic cases such as A.J. Miller could be met through the total savings reaped by a system of prevention. Reducing infant mortality is as important to our national health as fighting cancer, and it's far easier to achieve. No new medical breakthroughs are necessary. We only have to put into practice, on a national scale, techniques and programs that have been pioneered in places as disparate as Fort Wayne and San Diego, where Kenya Williams's son Miles is growing up healthy.

Ironically, Cindy's legislative victory in Indiana did not solve the Millers' problems. A few months later, Cindy got a new boss who was not sensitive to her need to work the evening shift so she could care for A.J. during the day while her husband was at work. She was told she had to work regular office hours, even though she had never been criticized for failing to perform her duties.

Searching for help, Cindy found that the cost of medically qualified child care for A.J. nearly equaled her take-home pay. She agonized over whether it was worth working for virtually nothing and having A.J. watched by baby-sitters, or whether she should risk leaving the job. In a meeting with the hospital administrator, she made her priorities clear: "My kids come first." The administrator remained inflexible, but Cindy did not want to fight Wabash Hospital, especially after what it had done to help A.J. She regretfully left her job as public relations director to stay home with A.J.

In Wabash, the 1992 recession hit hard. Layoffs at plants made jobs scarce, especially for a mother who needs to work at night. After looking for a job but finding no prospects, Cindy decided to stay home with A.J. for the time being. The family is now living on Tim's take-home earnings, about $26,000 a year. They have been forced to sell Cindy's car. They have no checking or savings accounts, no Christmas club, nothing to fall back on. A.J. is covered by Medicaid, but no one else in the family, even Nicholas, has health insurance.

The Millers are not alone. One in four Americans either has no health insurance or is insufficiently covered in case of a catastrophic illness. On average, they're working people like Tim and Cindy Miller.

For all they have received, the Millers are very grateful. Doing all that is humanly possible to keep themselves independent and self-sustaining, they are living on the edge of poverty, although to qualify for poverty status in the government's eyes, a family of four can only earn $13,924 a year. They have a house, a truck, life insurance, A.J. has Medicaid, and that's it.

A.J. was taken off oxygen at age two and a half—the week before Christmas in 1991—and off the apnea monitor the week after. Tall and skinny, without much hair, he jabbers a lot, loves music, and dances to Ricky Nelson crooning "Mary Lou." The eye damage caused by the exposure to oxygen has totally healed. He has no permanent brain damage; his lungs need to be strengthened, but they are expected to be normal. A.J. doesn't walk; he runs—an active, happy child. The occupational therapist estimates it will take two years before his fine-motor skills catch up with those of his age group, but Cindy is determined to help him become normal in every way. "Who can put a price on a human life?" she asks.

In 1990, the price of treating low-birthweight babies was $2 billion, according to the National Commission to Prevent Infant Mortality. The average hospital cost for a low-birthweight baby was $21,000, compared to $2,842 for a normal baby. Every year in the United States, nearly 300,000 low-birthweight babies are born and, tragically, 40,000 die before reaching their first birthday.

"Unless we act today, in the next thirteen years we will lose more American infants than we have lost soldiers in all the wars fought by the nation in this century," the commission pleaded in 1988. Its recommendations still go unheeded.

With good prenatal care and nutrition, low birthweight is largely preventable. But nearly 10 million children and 8.5 million mothers of childbearing age are not eligible for Medicaid* and cannot afford private insurance. America's market-driven health-care system seems almost perversely designed to prevent universal access.

In contrast, if we were to design the system for the benefit of expectant parents—who don't know if their baby will be born healthy or sick—the goal would be to provide an umbrella of coverage to help families maintain a stable financial situation and cope with their baby's needs. From the perspective of a newborn, who cannot choose its parents and cannot defend itself, the simple need is to guarantee access to health care.

Guaranteeing this right for newborns would be difficult and costly in the short term, but we can no longer afford a system that dooms babies and bankrupts their families. Health care for every mother and child would ultimately reduce infant mortality and lower medical and social costs over the course of their lifetimes. It would keep families together—and help babies like A.J. take their first baby steps on life's perilous journey.

* One recommendation of national health-care reform is to eliminate Medicaid as a separate and inferior system for the poor and to include uninsured children in mainstream "managed-care" systems. This may be beneficial if America's uninsured children receive truly equal and comprehensive coverage, but if all children are treated like Medicaid recipients today, it would be a tragic sacrifice of young lives for the sake of short-term cost savings.

EARLY CHILDHOOD

JESÚS CASTRO

The test of a nation's strength is the condition of its weakest and most vulnerable members. Five million children under age six in America are now in dire poverty—one of three children in major cities. In crime-infested neighborhoods, children live in decayed housing with lead paint peeling from the walls, rat droppings in the halls, broken windows on the stairways, and graffiti everywhere. They eat cheap, greasy junk food that makes them hyper and depletes their bodies. At the end of the month, when the welfare check runs out, they go without meals or scrounge for food in dumpsters. On their front stoops, they watch scenes of unspeakable violence, and there is no place where they can feel safe.

Yet they are children, and being children, they play amid the carnage; their laughter rings on the rusted fire escapes and echoes through grim streets where the only patches of color are murals dedicated to slain drug dealers. In bombed-out East New York, a section of Brooklyn where 109 homicides were reported within six square miles in 1990, boys pile rusted bedsprings on top of each other to create a makeshift trampoline. They bounce up and down on the bedsprings, executing front flips, back flips, soaring above the rubble. The potential of children flying head over heels above the broken springs seems infinite, but gravity brings them down to a neighborhood without hope.

In quiet suburbs, violence is hidden behind shutters, but Roberta Knowlton, who counsels teenagers in New Jersey's public schools, told me, "If any outside agent ever did to our kids what we're allowing to have happen to them, we would go to war against that country."

Eight in ten black children will be paupers before they're age eighteen, New York senator Daniel Patrick Moynihan estimates. Child poverty is as close as the nearest cheap motel, where people like twenty-seven-year-old Mary Rochester and her five hollow-eyed children are cramped in a fetid, single room. When I met them, the family had just been evicted from their apartment and slept the night before in a park in San Diego. There, the boys saw the flapping blankets of homeless men and thought they were ghosts. Put up in a motel by a church group, they wait alone in the room while Mary, who was battered by her common-law husband in Wisconsin and fled to California, wanders an avenue lined with hookers, debating whether she too should sell her body to feed her children.

It used to be an assumption of American life that every generation made sacrifices so that its children would be better off. But not today. Children are the poorest age group, and their income dropped by one-fifth during the 1980s. Meanwhile, the wealthiest group, aged 55 to 64, became even better off. Deadly childhood diseases that were once under control are now running rampant for lack of vaccines. At a suburban elementary school in southern California, the wall-ball court is named in memory of Hector López, who died of measles in 1990 after health officials said this country couldn't afford to vaccinate all children. The day Hector's mother buried him, her three other children were also in the hospital with measles. Twenty-nine thousand cases of measles were reported in 1990, and eighty-nine people died in what health officials called the largest outbreak in twenty years.

The family should act as a social immune system, shielding children from outside violence and abuse, but it too is breaking down. Today divorce is perhaps the most predictable crisis of childhood in America: Sixty percent of children born in 1987 will live in broken homes, a U.S. Census study estimates. Most of the 20 million children whose families divorce each year are middle-class. Such children are due child support, but fewer than half receive it in California, where $2.5 billion in child support payments went uncollected in 1992, according to the activist child-advocacy group Children Now. When a typical California family splits up, the absent parent's income rises 41 percent, while the income of the single parent and children typically plunges by 31 percent. National data show that 70 percent of absent parents have incomes at least twice as high as the poverty line.* Divorce provides an economic incentive for fathers to abandon children.

Even in middle-class homes where married parents both work, children with video games and trendy clothes suffer another kind of deprivation. They don't get enough time with their parents, who are working longer hours outside the home and depending more on institutional day care, latchkey programs, and television to raise their children. At a time when families most need public institutions to help them cope, children's programs are being cut back, often under pressure from taxpayers' groups that have little stake in children. Underpaid caretakers are poorly prepared to substitute for parents, and children hunger for parents' love and a secure home environ-

* Absent parents are usually men; single parents overwhelmingly are women. But sometimes caregiver roles are reversed. Generally, the single parent who takes care of the child and works has the hardest job—double duty.

ment to embrace them. Unlike previous eras when middle-class children were largely shielded from the instabil-
ity and violence of the poor (and the excesses of the rich),
the dangers facing today's children pervade our society,
threatening all classes.

Of all American children, those abandoned by their parents are the most vulnerable. To understand what it
means to be a defenseless child who is dependent on society for protection, consider the story of Jesús Castro, who
was forsaken by all.

Jesús was born healthy and seemingly normal in a Los
Angeles hospital in 1980, according to medical records of
his birth. But his parents were PCP addicts, and Jesús
was removed from their home in 1985 by the Department
of Children's Services because of a "failure to thrive." At
age five, he only weighed twenty-eight and a half pounds,
according to Robert Berke, a lawyer who later represented him.

After Jesús was removed, his father committed suicide
by hanging himself in jail, and his mother, distraught
over his death, killed herself within a month. The County
of Los Angeles became his guardian. In October 1985,
the county put Jesús in the custody of his grandparents,
even though authorities were warned of the potential
danger. Before Jesús's mother killed herself, she
informed a social worker that Jesús's step-grandmother
was abusive and his grandfather had a drinking problem
and became angry when drunk, Berke said. A social
worker from the Department of Children's Services was
supposed to visit him regularly, but typical caseloads were
so high (more than 75 children per social worker) that it
was impossible to monitor them all carefully. Four

months passed with no social worker checking on him, and subsequent visits did not find any problem.

During this period, Berke says Jesús was severely abused in his grandfather's house. In June 1986, eight months after Jesús was placed with his grandfather, police were summoned to the house by an anonymous call. They found a little boy lying unconscious in the mud by a backyard swimming pool as his step-grandmother sprayed him with a water hose. He had nearly drowned in the pool by accident, his step-grandmother claimed.

But authorities discovered evidence of abuse. His skin and genitals were covered with cigarette burns. He had been sodomized. He was paralyzed and partially blinded, and prosecutors later used the word "torture" to describe his suffering. Berke said Jesús's grandparents told a sheriff's deputy that Jesús was "a bad seed" and deserved repeated punishment. Jesús's grandfather was never charged with a crime, although his step-grandmother was convicted of child endangerment and served 300 days in jail.

After six months in the hospital, Jesús was placed in Lanterman Development Center, a state facility in Pomona that was ill-equipped to provide individual care to a spastic, quadriplegic child who was totally dependent. He breathed through a tube in his throat and digested food through a tube in his stomach. Curled in a fetal ball, unable to distinguish images or talk, he lived in a world of confusion and pain, utterly isolated. Nurses who fed and bathed him said they thought he recognized their voices, turning his head when they spoke. The smell of strawberries made him smile. But he was terrified of baths and cried when water touched his body. His fingers were permanently curled from disuse.

Jesús would have remained forgotten had Berke not

taken his case, sued Los Angeles County for physical and psychological damages, and won a $5 million jury award for his client. Although the suit was later overturned, money from an undisclosed settlement went to outfit a home for Jesús and other severely disabled foster children. But just as it was being completed, Jesús died of pneumonia at age eleven. (In a final irony, the Davis-Castro Home, outfitted for six disabled children, remained empty in 1992 because there wasn't enough money left from the settlement to operate it.)

The public furor over Jesús Castro's tragedy, which was given front-page coverage by the *Los Angeles Times,* coupled with concern over widespread neglect in the poorly administered foster-care system, led to a state investigation and shake-up of the children's agency. But the underlying causes of child abuse were not addressed by the investigation, or altered by the shuffling of officials. In Los Angeles, 33,000 children were in foster care—a small city of throwaways.

In 1990, I observed the children entering L.A.'s foster-care system. While a judge led me through the labyrinth of the Dependency Court, I noticed a little boy standing in an immense freight elevator and escorted by a guard who towered over him. No older than six, the child was dressed in a white shirt with a bright red bow tie. It looked as if a butterfly had landed beneath his chin, but the corners of his mouth were pulled down, tautly trembling. His eyes were filled with fear as he gazed upward at the adult strangers. I was struck by the gulf between that child, all alone, bravely trying to keep from crying, and the judge and lawyers talking about other court cases. Privacy laws prevented me from ever learning the little boy's name, so I shall call him Cecil as I follow him, and thousands of other children, through the court.

Three days after being removed from home and placed

in a children's shelter, without a chance to see his parents, Cecil is bused into the cavernous basement of the Criminal Courts Building in downtown L.A. Wide-eyed, he watches manacled prisoners being marched through the same caged sally port where killers are brought to court. In a dim waiting room, Cecil joins other frightened kids watching cartoons on TV. The court dockets are overwhelmed with foster cases, and the corridor outside of the courtrooms is jammed with hundreds of families, standing and waiting. With a thousand new children entering the system each month, the court docket is so crowded that children's fates—whether they would be returned home or be separated, perhaps forever, from their parents—are typically decided in ten-minute legal proceedings that are charades of justice.

Waiting four hours until his case is called, Cecil isn't permitted to see his parents until they are facing each other in the courtroom. Bruised and battered by a stepfather, but still wanting his mother's love, he can't speak for himself but is represented by a lawyer who doesn't remember his name—the same lawyer who represents the county. This is a conflict of interest because Cecil's need for social services is in conflict with the county's need to cut them. His mother is represented by a frazzled, court-appointed attorney who is so overloaded with clients that he met her for the first time a few minutes earlier in the hall. A robed judge, high up, fiddles through papers and peers down at the terrified child and his parents. With a few unintelligible words, the gavel comes down and Cecil is led away from his weeping mother into the labyrinthine courthouse, which now stands between him and his family. The next time many children like Cecil return, they will be in shackles: One in four children in California's juvenile justice system started out in the foster-care system. Many will be remanded to the custody of the state for as long as they live.

In 1990, there were 50,000 young souls caught in the limbo of L.A. Dependency Court. Presiding judge Paul Boland, who was planning a new child-oriented court-house in suburban L.A., was so disturbed by the overpop-ulated system that he frankly told me that judges were sentencing drug addicts to therapies that were not avail-able, all because of cuts in social services. While they waited for treatment that didn't come, their children were kept in foster homes that, in some cases, were more dangerous than their own homes. Horror stories abounded. The system was literally consuming children under its care like a monster in a Greek tragedy.

Across the country, New York City has an equally large population of foster children. Huge increases are also reported in Michigan, Illinois, and other states. Nationwide, half a million children are reported in out-of-home placement, with explosive increases of children in child welfare, juvenile justice, and mental health sys-tems, according to a 1989 congressional inquiry. The Select Committee on Children, Youth, and Families esti-mated that the number of children in out-of-home place-ment, expected to increase by 73 percent, will grow to 840,000 by 1995. Because new children are constantly entering and leaving foster care, jails, and mental hospi-tals, the number of children who at one time or another are totally dependent on the state as their guardians rises to the millions. The committee described the situa-tion as "alarming," with "extraordinary failings" in the child welfare and juvenile justice systems.

But the committee's 1989 report, "No Place to Call Home: Discarded Children in America," also found rea-son to hope. Relying on expert witnesses who testified before Congress, it documented that prevention and early intervention programs were beneficial and cost-effective. Family preservation programs counsel abusive parents on nonviolent child-rearing techniques, help children heal and regain trust, and guide families to work through their problems together so that children can live at home in a safe environment. In Utah and Washington State, where family preservation was pioneered, 68 percent of the children who got help early remained in their homes or with relatives, the committee reported. In Maryland, only 2 percent of families who got intensive services required out-of-home placement, saving about $6,000 per child. In Virginia, family preservation cost $1,214 per child, about one-tenth the amount spent on foster care and a twentieth the cost of residential care.

Despite these life- and cost-saving examples reflecting a sensible agenda of child-welfare reform, the report on discarded children was shelved by Congress, and the committee's recommendations were lost in the partisan battles on Capitol Hill.

But most children depend on their families, not the government, for protection. And the revolution in family structure, along with rising child poverty and deficit-starved governments, has made America's children more vulnerable than ever. For children living in single-parent families—their generation's new plurality—the issue of child support is crucial. Today, more children depend on the child-support system than on any other institution except the public schools. The failure of child support endangers children of all classes. The poorest children fall into the toils of welfare, and middle-class children hover on the brink of poverty.

Senator Daniel Patrick Moynihan of New York has studied the relationship between family structure and poverty for four decades, and his work reveals the dangers facing America's children. In the mid-1960s, Moynihan, then assistant secretary of labor, was the first to report the breakdown of the black family; in the 1990s, he is concerned about the breakdown of *all* families. He believes the economic status of children, and their hope of succeeding as adults, depends more on their family structure than on race or class. America faces what he calls a "new social condition," stemming from the rise of the single-parent family.

Single-parent family is not an oxymoron, but it is a difficult way to grow up. From a child's point of view, it matters very much that one's father or mother is missing, even if the other parent does everything possible to make up for the lack. The emotional impact of growing up in a single-parent family is multiplied by the financial consequences. "Nearly one third—30.2 percent of all children—are paupers before attaining their majority," Moynihan wrote in 1991. "Not a pretty word; but not a pretty condition."

Because most single-parent families are headed by women, it has become popular for politicians to blame women, particularly poor teenage mothers, for bringing children into poverty and keeping them there, generation after generation. But men who skip out on child-support payments aren't held responsible for their children's suffering.

The plight of Lynn and Lori Speir, whose parents divorced when they were toddlers, and who received no child support until they were in their teens, reflects the fate of millions of middle-class children thrust into virtual poverty by their parents' breakup. Their father, Scott Speir, an army veteran who owned a small business that made dental appliances in Long Beach, California, walked out on their mother, Susan, in 1973. They divorced two years later. Susan was given custody and responsibility for raising her daughters; a judge ordered their father to pay $100 a month for each child.

But Scott never paid child support, and Susan was forced to live off her $500 monthly take-home pay as a secretary. Out of this sum, she had to pay a $225 mortgage, far lower than today's rates, and another $200 for child care so that she could work. That left her only $75 a month to pay for basic utilities, food, and doctor's bills, according to Susan's account published in the July 1990 issue of *Ladies' Home Journal.*

After her meek requests for child support, her ex-husband began harassing her: "Go on, beg," he taunted. "I want to hear you beg."

Desperate, Susan tried to get authorities to enforce the divorce settlement, but Scott moved to Tennessee. By the time California sent petition papers to Nashville, Scott had moved to Illinois, then Arizona, and finally Texas. The search for him was exhausting, and Susan found herself so involved with secretarial work, child-support paperwork, and bills that she barely had time for her daughters, who had holes in their shoes and hand-me-down clothing. She could barely afford essentials, let alone extras like movies or trips to the zoo.

Frustrated at the inability of the system to provide minimal child support for her daughters, Susan decided to start a support group for families in her situation. She called it SPUNK—Single Parents United 'N Kids—and the organization grew rapidly. While Susan was helping another SPUNK mother in court, she caught the attention of a Los Angeles deputy district attorney, Don Gerecht. The DA's office filed felony charges against Scott for not paying child support, and he was arrested in

Texas. Magically, Scott paid the $13,761 he owed. He visited his daughters once after that, but never contacted them again. In 1987, they received word that he had died.

Fifteen million American children are currently living without their fathers, and half of them are due child support, the Bureau of the Census estimates. Three-fifths of the children with absent fathers are white, and the percentage of absent white fathers has doubled since 1960, following the trend of most black children who grow up without fathers at home. Youth crime, drugs, and poor school performance are all linked to the absence of fathers from children's lives. This amounts to a nationwide abandonment of paternity.

Grass-roots organizations like SPUNK, which now serves 3,000 families a year, sprouted up across the country and joined together to form the National Child Support Advocacy Coalition. Susan Speir, who has served as the coalition's president, was among thousands of mothers who lobbied Congress for passage of the Family Support Act of 1988. The law, sponsored by Senator Moynihan, requires employers to withhold the wages of all parents who owe child support on or after January 1, 1994. But it fell short of creating a national child-support system, Susan believes.

"More women are realizing that they can—and should—stand up for what rightfully belongs to them and their children," she says. "After all, as my own case proves, you can fight the system and win."

In spite of grass-roots efforts and tightening of federal law, millions of absent parents still avoid payment. Most single parents don't have the resources to fight red tape in local bureaucracies, and many lose.

Poor children who are dependent on public child support are the most savagely treated. Freezes and cuts in Aid to Families with Dependent Children (AFDC) reduced children's welfare income by 39 percent, after discounting inflation, from 1972 to 1990, according to Wendell Primus, a congressional budget analyst. Welfare reform efforts such as Workfare, which forces mothers to take menial jobs in order to get their child-support benefits (as if raising children was not valuable work), may help some women gain work experience, but only by taking valuable time and energy away from their children.

The emotional debate over welfare becomes even clearer when it is discussed in terms of child support. Most Americans believe that both parents should support children, but our system doesn't work that way. Seventy percent of never-married fathers escape paying child support because paternity was never established. Welfare encourages parents to break up and keeps children below the poverty line. Poor children pauperized by welfare, and middle-class children cheated out of child support, are harmed by society's inability to provide social insurance for divorce. Family breakup becomes a catastrophe for millions of American children today.

The same destructive system that denies sufficient child support also dictates that millions of children get inadequate health care. Welfare and Medicaid regulations are so punitive in some states that they break up families and rob children of their father's presence. Tennessee, for example, generally forbids families with two able-bodied parents to receive public assistance and Medicaid. This policy had a disastrous effect on the Baskin family in Nashville, and especially on their beautiful, blond-haired boy Kevin.

His mother, Gayle Baskin, still speaks with tears in her eyes about the day in 1982 when her son Kevin, then three months old, struck the soft spot of his head against the edge of his rocker and stopped breathing. Her husband, Eddie Baskin, was tending Kevin, and when he saw the baby turning blue, he desperately shook him and did mouth-to-mouth resuscitation. By the time they got Kevin to the hospital, doctors said he'd suffered a cerebral hemorrhage, and he was hospitalized for three weeks. Initially Kevin appeared to be normal, but by age five he was suffering emotional disturbances. His parents, hardworking people with minimum-wage jobs, could not afford private psychiatric care for him. One day Mrs. Baskin found that her son had hanged himself with a rope until his face was blue. In school, he banged his head on the wall and couldn't be controlled by teachers.

At age six, after a second suicide attempt, Kevin was admitted to a psychiatric hospital and diagnosed with acute depression and learning disabilities. Treatment at the hospital was $28,000 a month. Mr. Baskin, who worked for $6 an hour, six days a week as a grave digger at Woodlawn Cemetery, didn't have health insurance to pay for Kevin's ongoing psychiatric care. Mrs. Baskin, who quit her job at a five-and-dime to take care of Kevin and his two siblings, decided to go on welfare in order to apply for Medicaid. So, in order to get Kevin treatment, the Baskins faced a wrenching choice. Either Mr. Baskin would have to abandon his wife and three children at the time when they needed him most, or he would have to break the law and stay at home, hiding from the welfare inspectors.

In the kitchen one night, Mrs. Baskin cried bitterly to her husband, "Eddie, it's not fair! This is a family that loves each other and the government makes you do things you don't want to do."

"I don't know what else to do," Eddie replied.

The next morning, he complied with the law and moved out. Kevin was hospitalized for four months and discharged after Medicaid stopped paying for his treatment, even though his mother said he wasn't any better.

Back home, his psychological condition remained unstable, and he was prone to violent, self-destructive outbursts. Kevin's experience with America's inadequate mental health system was typical: More than 70 percent of emotionally disturbed children received inappropriate mental health services, or none at all, the Select Congressional Committee on Children, Youth, and Families reported in 1989.

When I visited Nashville in the fall of 1990, Eddie was sleeping in a garage at Woodlawn Cemetery and coming home to visit his family for an hour at dinner. Kevin, who needed his father more than ever, was not able to call him at night.

"We love each other," Mrs. Baskin told me in a depressed voice, gesturing to a Santa Claus poster hung on the door of her clean but dirt-poor living room in a Nashville housing project. Kevin had spent last Christmas in the hospital, and she prayed he would be at home for this one. Her deepest regret was that her husband couldn't be with his family. She explained, "It's not us wanting to separate. It's the stupid law. The government don't want to give you anything, and they don't want you to have anything either, if that makes any sense. If Eddie moves back in, we'd lose Medicaid and food stamps and Kevin won't get the treatment he needs."

At night, gunshots rang out in the high-crime neighborhood where drug needles lay scattered in the weeds. Alone in the housing project with her children, all Gayle Baskin could do was cry "Get down!" so they wouldn't be hit by a stray bullet.

In 1992, Kevin was officially designated as learning disabled. This entitled him to receive $422 a month from Supplemental Security Income (SSI), which automatically made him eligible for Medicaid health coverage, and to attend a special-education school. Mr. Baskin could now come home without fearing that Kevin's Medicaid would be canceled, but by this time the separation had taken a toll on his and Gayle's marriage; Eddie had moved from the cemetery garage to his sister's house. Kevin, who was just starting to improve at age nine, was deeply disturbed that his father wasn't living at home. Gayle found a duplex in a quiet neighborhood outside the projects and hoped that by moving there, she could protect her children and undo the damage to her marriage. "If I get out from under the government, we can breathe better and get my family together," she said.

Although the multiple problems besetting families such as the Baskins can't be blamed solely on the government, it's clear that family-busting regulations make everything worse for children. As the Millers had discovered in Indiana, welfare bureaucrats think nothing of telling parents to get a divorce to qualify for Medicaid, even though this violates not only the spirit of the law but the letter of new federal regulations that attempt to prevent such horror stories. When the message comes down from the highest level of government that people who apply for benefits are to be scrutinized as welfare frauds and cheats, officials on all levels are tempted to treat applicants in the most abrupt and abusive manner possible. The ultimate victims are children.

The interlocking crises of child poverty, divorce, disease, violence, and abandonment are symptoms of a pervasive devaluation of children in our culture. Any one of these trends by itself would be bad for children. But together they show a portrait of a generation under attack from every direction. Many of the most disadvantaged children have multiple problems: A foster child may come from a divorced family, have health problems, and experience poverty. In this 360-degree free-fire zone, children don't have a chance.

To gauge the extent of our children's impoverishment during the 1980s, the Joint Center for Political and Economic Studies in Washington looked at the poverty rate for U.S. families with children and compared it to rates for our major European allies. The results: During the 1980s, almost 24 percent of U.S. households with children were below the poverty line—a figure nearly twice that of our allies. In the case of our closest economic competitor, West Germany before reunification, less than 8 percent of households with children were poor—one-third the U.S. poverty rate.

Thus, while hundreds of thousands of U.S. troops protected German children from the nonexistent Soviet Union, American children confronted destructive forces within our society—and from a government that is indifferent if not hostile.*

---

* President Clinton promises to strengthen the child-support system and reform AFDC in order to "end welfare as we know it." Programs that provide single parents with education, job training, and health care so that they can get jobs and support their families are laudable. But previous welfare reforms have had punitive effects on children, and Clinton's proposals must be monitored to make sure that they don't have unintended negative effects.

CHILDHOOD

COCOONING BUTTERFLIES

While the declining fortunes of America's children should be starkly visible to all, Americans who care deeply about our children are pioneering ways to help young people and their families take small steps toward a healthier life. Interlocking crises of child poverty, neglect, and abuse, which trap millions of children beneath America's collapsing family structure, provide a crucial opportunity to help kids, support families, and heal society.

In dozens of child-development centers, schools, family groups, and community organizations from Auburn, Washington, to Brooklyn, New York, professionals are developing practical techniques for dealing with the devastating array of social, economic, physical, and psychological problems confronting America's children. In hundreds of grass-roots programs in every corner of America, thousands of caregivers and parents are trying out these techniques, adapting them to their children's needs, and refining them within their communities. Pitted against the enormous devastation, their efforts are small, halting, and of limited success. But in the shadow of our children's presumptive doom, these Americans have planted seeds of hope that children can be nurtured and grow up to their full potential, even in toxic cocoons of violence and poverty.

There is no way to prove it, but from visits to child-development centers and schools, and from talks with children, families, and experts in the field, a consensus view emerges that, for every socially created problem that causes children to suffer, someone has developed a preventive or healing technique somewhere in America. The tools, methods, and services are often fragmented, specialized, costly, or inaccessible, but they have been shown effective in helping some children, some of the time.

In America, each generation reinvents childhood. Yet children's basic needs of love, security, order, and protection do not change. The most sequential programs help children find new ways to fulfill these age-old needs. The programs are comprehensive and sequential, beginning before birth and following the child's growth to school and beyond. They nurture the whole child's development—physical, cognitive, emotional, and social—and support parents struggling to fend for their families.

Peg Mazen of Auburn, Washington, is helping young children from broken families overcome grave disabilities and move forward in their development, while helping their poor, uneducated parents progress from government dependency to self-reliance. The Families First program that Peg directs provides comprehensive services to the children of 120 families living in the Seattle area. Most of the families are headed by single white women, and all of them are poor—the population that has been stigmatized as "welfare dependents." Families First is part of a massive five-year, $125 million federal demonstration project in twenty-four sites scattered around the country. Sponsored by liberal Senator Edward Kennedy of Massachusetts and initially run by the conservative Bush administration, the Comprehensive Child Development Program is the largest experiment in the United States that combines child development and family support.

A crucial tenet of Families First is that families define

themselves and are not confined to the traditional family configuration. Thus native Americans living on the Muckeshoot reservation can define their family differently than single mothers living in suburban Seattle.

The program culminates over twenty-five years of research in early intervention programs, beginning with Project Head Start in 1965. A product of the War on Poverty, Head Start was the first national child-development program for the disadvantaged to survive and gain recognition from both liberals and conservatives. The premise of Head Start is simple: If you help disadvantaged children three to five years old prepare for school, they will enter kindergarten better able to learn, develop, and compete. It invests in child development—not government handouts—as the core of an antipoverty strategy.

Much of the supporting evidence for Head Start's success comes from a study of 123 black youths enrolled in the Perry Preschool program in Ypsilanti, Michigan. The study, which tracked the youths to age nineteen, demonstrates that intensive preschool programs improve mental performance, scholastic placement, and achievement in school; increase the rates of high school graduation and higher education; decrease delinquency and crime; and reduce welfare assistance and teenage pregnancy. The Select Congressional Committee on Children, Youth, and Families estimates that $1 invested in quality preschool education saves $4.75 in lower costs of special education, public assistance, and crime.

However, Head Start is no panacea for the devastating problems facing children and families. First, it only reached about 620,000 children in 1992—about one-fourth of those who are eligible and would benefit from preschool nurturing, according to the National Commission on Children. Congress estimates that to provide every income-eligible child with at least two years of Head Start would cost $7.66 billion in 1994.

Second, Head Start has a serious flaw: Providing children milk, cookies, and healthy nurturing for a few hours a day doesn't affect the conditions in which the child lives outside the Head Start center. Children's difficulties are rooted in the problems of their parents, and Head Start has few resources to help parents deal with the Sisyphean difficulties that poor and working-class families confront in trying to provide basic food, shelter, clothing, stimulation, health care, and a safe environment for their children. Furthermore, because many developmental problems are linked to prenatal drug use and early neglect, Dr. Toni Linder, an associate professor of education at the University of Denver and a specialist in early child development, says, "Head Start is too late for many children."

Peg Mazen got involved in Head Start early in her career. She grew frustrated seeing children make advances in preschool, only to be thwarted and wounded as their families floundered in poverty in neighborhoods of violence. She shifted her work to provide social services for adults, only to watch children being dealt with as appendages by the system. Instinctively, she wanted to link services for children and families, but the bureaucratic divisions at every level of government, which cut families into pieces labeled by problems, prevented any one agency from dealing with the whole child in relation to family and community.

In 1986, a pioneering program in the crime-ridden Robert Taylor housing project of Chicago showed that a comprehensive, community-centered approach helped children develop, breathing life into a devastated neighborhood that consumed children and their families. Nicknamed the "Beethoven Project," the Center for

Successful Child Development combined two strategies: (1) community participation in the choice, planning, and delivery of services, and (2) a family-centered rather than a child-centered approach.

This commonsense melding of child-development and family-support programs became the core of the federal Comprehensive Child Development Program—in concept. Recognizing that the common failing of federal programs is their central planning and bureaucratic inflexibility, each of the twenty-four demonstration projects is given leeway to design its own means for delivering services. However, all must provide child development, preschool education, child care, health, nutrition, adult education, and employment services. The projects range from rural Appalachia to seaside Miami Beach to urban Brooklyn, helping children in remote Fort Totten, North Dakota, and trendy Venice, California.

In Auburn, Washington, a sprawling suburban area near Seattle, Peg Mazen leaped at the opportunity to create a continuous, comprehensive approach to helping children and families develop. Instead of families with multiple problems being forced to seek help in different agencies spread over the sprawling suburban area, counselors go to the family's home, observing children and helping parents develop a long-term economic and health plan for their families.

"What are your dreams for your children?" the home visitor asks. "How are we going to realize them together?"

Mazen's approach is to build on families' strengths, not their pathologies and weaknesses, to embolden parents to think beyond daily emergencies to larger goals and provide steps to reach them. Little achievements and accomplishments are crucial to a child's development, and to a parent's self-worth. There is an analogy between a child climbing up a jungle gym, learning developmental skills, and a family learning to progress from welfare dependency to self-reliance.

If one compares the stages of life to steps running up a staircase, from birth to old age, then the stages of development through infancy and childhood are the first set of stairs. But many children can't even crawl onto the first step because they have disabilities that began before birth. For others growing up in deprived circumstances, development is delayed and they are held back at every step until they get stuck far below their potential— frozen in poverty. Many have developmental problems that could be easily conquered, but they live in precarious families that falter on the stairs. They need a railing to guide them upward . . . But in America today, the railing is missing or broken, and the stairs are designed so that one must fall all the way down before getting any help.

The development analogy is a powerful model for the struggle of children and families to climb to a better way of life. It is a far more compelling vision of how humans grow than the bootstrap metaphor of Horatio Alger myth, and it is a more humane vision than the economic determinist models of Adam Smith and Karl Marx. It provides the first step toward a reconstructive vision of society based on natural processes of human growth and development.

These abstractions are grounded in practical methods used in child-development centers. At the child-care facility run by Families First, there are three separate rooms for infants, toddlers, and preschoolers. A time-lapse image of their development shows them slowly blooming from gurgling babies to careening toddlers to concentrated preschoolers.

Parents participate at the center, actively learning to nurture and discipline their kids in ways that don't demean and hurt them. For many parents who were brutalized or neglected as children, parenting classes and hands-on experience are crucial to prevent abuse from being passed down to the next generation.

Families First's annual budget of $1.3 million amounts to about $15,000 per family: less than the cost of hospital-izing one premature infant in intensive care for two weeks, or placing one child and teenage mother in foster care for a year. Cynics say it would be better to give poor families $15,000 a year and let them spend it how they wish, but most taxpayers oppose such handouts. And, in fact, most kids' problems cannot be solved by giving their parents money alone, without providing a means to help them deal with underlying problems.

Reducing government dependency is a prime objective. Through the work of a full-time employment counselor, one-third of the parents in the program are now working or in job training or college; one-third are working on lit-eracy and high school equivalency; and one-third are working full-time on family and human development issues, staying home and raising their children.

To evaluate the program, the 120 families in Families First will be compared to a control group of 120 other families who get no services from Families First but are still eligible for entitlements—if they can get them from overwhelmed public agencies. The five-year experiment will end in the mid-1990s, when costs and benefits will be compared by an independent inspector hired by the fed-eral government.

Another community-based model of child development and family support is flourishing in the Sunset Park neighborhood of Brooklyn, New York. Rather than being created from the top down by the federal government, it is a program growing from the grass roots up. Sunset

Park has a population of more than 100,000 people, predominately poor and Latino, with one-third of its residents under the age of eighteen. Over the past sixteen years, the Center for Family Life, a nonprofit institution founded by two Roman Catholic nuns, has recreated a sense of small-town community, with the family and the school at its heart. The center provides full-time child care, after-school programs, counseling, food, health, foster care, and employment services. The nuns resist any effort to label people by their problems or exclude anyone because of income. In an age of shortages, they have accomplished an extraordinary feat: All programs are available, free of charge, to anyone who lives in the neighborhood. They are staffed by a small group of professionals and dozens of volunteers from the community.

Sunset Park is a low-income neighborhood of rowhouses fronted by stoops overlooking bleak streets, with the attendant urban problems of drugs, domestic violence, and poverty. It was known as a place where immigrants landed, families fended for themselves, children were wooed by drugs, and no one belonged. When the nuns drew a circle around Sunset Park in 1978, they were making a commitment to build a community that would, in the words of its founders, "embrace and take responsibility for its families." Largely through the efforts of the center, which involves thousands of families in programs from birth to old age, Sunset Park has been transformed into a community where people feel they belong and are able to help each other. Radiating from the Center for Family Life is hope—not the easy hope that a magic pill will solve all problems, but the hard hope that with tenacity, inventiveness, discipline, and a great deal of love, children's lives can be bettered, their families strengthened, and community rekindled in the alienating darkness.

There is hope for Felipe, a six-year-old child being raised by relatives in the community. Exposed to drugs in the womb, Felipe endured his first year in the chaotic world of his crack-addicted mother, suffering extreme neglect. Abandoned by her, he was taken in by his aunt, who began raising him along with her two natural children. But Felipe had difficulty getting along with them— or with anyone. Trying to raise a hyperactive crack baby almost broke up his aunt's marriage. When it came time to put him in school, he was impossible to control. The public school counselor wanted to test him, and the expectation was that he would be labeled developmentally deficient, sent to a special-education school, and isolated with other stigmatized children who had developmental problems and poor expectations. In New York City, with thousands of children lost in the social service system, Felipe had little hope.

But Felipe was referred to Sisters Mary Paul and Geraldine at the Center for Family Life. A counselor went home and met with his aunt in her apartment; together, they created a plan not only for Felipe, but for his family. He was not labeled and segregated, but put in an after-school program with other children, where he participated in a small therapy group. Felipe started out kicking and biting everyone. But the center helped his aunt and teachers break through Felipe's raging defenses and reach the little boy. They made it clear to Felipe that they would not tolerate his tantrums, but instead of demanding that he repress his feelings, they helped him find words to express them. They set expectations that Felipe would succeed—not fail—and he pushes those expectations to the limits.

"There is a tendency to eliminate this kind of child— everyone wants him somewhere else," says Sister

Geraldine. She refuses to segregate him as a problem child; instead, she includes him in activities whenever possible, while making sure he is supervised.

For example, the center hires teenagers to work in the after-school program. The little kids relate to the older ones, who faced similar problems at home and on the street. Felipe, who has no father figure, responds to the teenage boy who reads to him. He gets plenty of individual attention before he is moved into the main group. There, he sees his neighbors and friends as staff members and participants in the program. His aunt comes in to talk with the group leader about his problems in class. Immigrant families don't have the English-language skills or the confidence to ask for help from schools. The program helps develop relationships between parents and teachers, children and school, school and community.

If one approach fails, the center tries another. Suppose Felipe's aunt says she no longer can take care of him. The center is already working to find his real mother and bring her back, although this is kept secret. Felipe knows there's another woman he calls his aunt, but doesn't know she is his real mother. She is in drug therapy, and at one point she may be able to take care of him. Until then, Felipe would be put in foster care with a family in his community. There would be joint sessions with the foster mother, natural mother, aunt, family counselor, and Felipe. He would stay in the same school with the same counselors and not lose his family.

"Part of what we give the child is to give back their parents," says Sister Mary Paul, who cofounded the center in 1978 and helps raise its $2 million budget.

Against the dangers facing children like Felipe, the victories the center achieves seem small. Felipe was so hyperactive in the beginning that he couldn't concentrate or stand still, much less participate in organized activities. But he slowly began to come around. In the Christmas show, Sister Geraldine watched him walk down the aisle dressed in an angel outfit and carrying a battery-powered candle. The glow on his face was her reward.

Every day presents a new catastrophe, a new challenge. This day, Sister Mary Paul gets a call that a girl has come to school with bruises. Her mother, recently widowed by a drug-related slaying in Puerto Rico, is punishing the child because she won't eat and get dressed in time for school. Authorities want to remove the girl from her mother's home, but Sister Mary Paul convinces them to let her stay with her mother—on the condition that she stop beating the child, who is depressed by the death of her father. Counselors are helping the family grieve nonviolently, and pull together.

Children's problems do not end when they start school; rather they bring a whole new host of problems with them to class. America's public schools are overwhelmed with children who are hungry, disoriented, angry, tired, poorly cared for, sexually abused, drug-exposed, out of control, neglected, and abandoned. Those from broken, chaotic homes have difficulty focusing in their classes and do poorly in school. When they fail academically, failure becomes the template for later failures in jobs and relationships.

Americans fear that our education system is failing, and they have been convinced that big social experiments don't work, are a tremendous waste of money, and cause more problems than they solve. But most Americans still entrust their children to the public schools, and they are innovating small programs that can work in surprising ways, at low cost, with minimal waste, and with great potential for doing good.

A program that enables children and parents to use the public schools for their benefit—rather than the reverse—was designed by a professor of psychiatry at Yale University, Dr. James Comer. As a black psychiatrist, Dr. Comer believed that one of the reasons African-American children fail in school was that the schools failed to acknowledge the emotional and social needs of children coming from minority backgrounds. His psychological background taught him that nurturing children's character development was as important—and as legitimate—a role for schools as teaching academics. In fact, without developmental supports, children were bound to fail.

Yet child development alone could not make schools serve children's needs, Comer believed, unless the family and the community were involved in the process. As a member of a strong, success-oriented black family (Comer's mother raised five children who all graduated from college), he cited the important relationships that developed in the poor but socially intact black community of East Chicago, Indiana, where he grew up as the child of a steelworker in the 1940s. But urban schools in New Haven, Connecticut, were administrative fiefdoms run by suburban outsiders who were cut off culturally and economically from the lives of inner-city students; the resulting isolation was devastating to children's education.

Working in New Haven schools for two decades, Dr. Comer patiently developed a model of education where parents were brought into classrooms and shared in the administration of schools. Teachers were encouraged to get involved with children's lives at home and within the community. The Comer model develops relationships between children, families, and educators. Each school has a mental-health team, a parents' group, and a governance and management team including all members of the school community—the principal, teachers, mental health workers, and parents.

"The idea that teachers are 'parent surrogates' for their students doesn't sit well with many people, though most find the notion of teachers as child developers less troublesome," Comer wrote in the National Education Association's journal. "But when we consider the fact that good child-rearing and child-development practices promote academic learning, the notion of teacher as parent surrogate becomes logical. In fact, many of the techniques and conditions required for successful parenting in families are also required for successful teaching in school."

Comer schools were pioneered among the almost wholly minority population of New Haven, but the concept is spreading to other parts of the country. In Leavenworth, Kansas, a predominately white community situated amidst nine prisons—federal, state, military, and local—the schools were undergoing great stress from discipline problems when the district adopted the Comer plan.

Stephanie Smith, a thirty-one-year-old elementary school teacher in Leavenworth, was sent to a Comer training program at Yale University. There she learned basic tools and gained a vocabulary to name the problems she'd been exposed to in the classroom, and she discovered a method to identify problems and solve them.

"It created a different atmosphere of partnership in the school," Stephanie says. "There are a lot of dinosaurs and elephants in the field. They want to stand up and give curriculum and have students be tape recorders. The Comer model says this is a whole child and we want to nurture all parts of them."

After returning to her elementary school, Stephanie had a clearer idea that children's behavior problems in class stemmed from deeper problems at home. Instead of viewing the children as failures, she marveled that they had survived to come to school each morning.

Stephanie was walking down a corridor one day when a redheaded third grader started screaming obscenities at the top of his voice. She noticed the same child sitting in the principal's office day after day, unable to remain in the classroom because he was out of control.

Stephanie asked the principal to give her a fourth-grade class the next year, in order to put that child in her room. She wanted to work with him, because nothing upset her more than to hear adults talking about a child and saying there was nothing they could do to stop that kid from winding up in Leavenworth Prison.

Mike, the redheaded problem child, was unkempt, with wild, curly hair and angry, burning eyes. At nine he was notorious as the meanest boy in school, so brutal that no matter what he did, the other children never made fun of him, because they were terrified. He had no control of his bladder and wet himself in class. Stephanie soon learned that Mike got the brunt of his alcoholic father's rages at home. If Mike wet his bed, his father forced him to sit all evening on a stool in a locked room.

Mike had been failing before he reached Stephanie's class—partly, she believed, because the teaching style of his third-grade teacher was unstructured. Children who are out of control often need strong, consistent discipline, and Stephanie's style of teaching was to be very strict, while showing Mike she cared about him unconditionally.

She showed her caring when she made a trip to Texas, leaving her class with a substitute teacher who was briefed on Mike's behavior. She made a deal with him before she left. If he behaved, she would bring him back a special gift from Texas, but if he misbehaved, she instructed the teacher to call her long distance—and the cost of the call would constitute his present. Stephanie had made it to the last day of her trip when she got a call.

"Oh, Miss Smith," Mike said in a wavering voice. She asked him why he was calling, and he said he wasn't behaving and the principal wanted to suspend him. "Well, I already bought you the gift," she said. "I have no choice but to not give it to you." Mike said sadly, "I know." Stephanie heard the regret in his voice and responded with a proposal. "There are two and a half hours left of school. If you settle down and are still in school Monday morning, I'll give you the gift."

By the grace of the substitute teacher, Mike was there on Monday. Every day, Mike tested Stephanie's patience, but she saw that this was his way of finding out if she really cared about him. At home, there was no stable family life. Mike's mother had abandoned the family and gone to Florida, and his stepmother had four different children by three different fathers.

"No matter what you do, I love you," Stephanie said to Mike, time after time. "I'm gonna stand here and be the wall you run into—or the force that lifts you up."

The first twenty-three times she said this, it didn't make any sense to him. But the turning point in their relationship, she believes, was one Valentine's Day when she was walking down the hall. "I love you," she whispered. Mike passed her, but she heard him whisper to her back, "I know you do."

Mike began dressing more neatly, combing his hair, and showing he cared about his appearance. He learned how to express his feelings to other children with words, instead of striking out with his fists. His newfound self-control and physical prowess won him friends in class, and he underwent a social transformation. At the end of fourth grade he was voted the most popular boy in his class. He still lagged in academics, however. He flunked every spelling test except the last one, when he got a C+.

When Mike went into fifth grade, Stephanie briefed the teacher about him and said that whenever Mike got out of control, she would be available to help out. Mike ended up spending many a day back in Stephanie's class. If he was disruptive in assemblies, she would flash hand signs across the room, and he would quiet down and sign back.

A key principle of the Comer model is to get parents involved in school. Mike's father, an avid hunter and fisherman, disparaged book learning until he was invited to demonstrate his outdoor abilities in the school. He showed children how to bait a hook and locate rainbow trout lurking in a stream, and this demonstration subtly changed the way he related to school.

Stephanie maintained her commitment to Mike by requesting a transfer to sixth grade in order to have Mike once again in her class. Having continuity in his life at school helped make up for the lack of it at home, and Mike showed steady improvement in his behavior as well as his studies. But sometimes he lapsed. One day, he threw an assignment paper on Stephanie's desk in a disrespectful way. Stephanie yanked his desk over her head and carried it out into the hall. She ordered Mike to carry his chair out there and stay until he was ready to show proper respect. Fifteen minutes later, he appeared at the door. She smiled and asked Mike to come in.

"I'm sorry," he said.

"Thank you, Mike," Stephanie told him. "I'm honored that you showed you cared."

The extraordinary commitment of this teacher for Mike can hardly be considered a practical goal for all teachers and schools. But the Comer model, which empowers a teacher to go to the limits, also supports creative partnerships between other teachers, administrators, parents, and students. So far, it has been adopted by more than 100 schools in nine districts in eight states. The Rockefeller Foundation has awarded the Comer program a $15 million grant to expand further. What is most essential is that it fosters a community of learning.

Caring for children at risk is the hallmark of a special Pupil Advocate Program for young black males in the San Diego public schools. When it was found that black male students tested consistently lower and had a higher dropout rate than all other groups, the school district hired four young African-American men to act as role models for black boys.

Like the Comer program, the pupil advocates concentrated on human development and building alliances with the families of the boys. They taught African history and culture, nurtured self-esteem and respect, and showed black children the achievements of Africans, such as Aesop, whose ancient fables are world famous.

Hannibal was a muscular eleven-year-old boy who was bright, witty, and precocious by nature. He was also extremely assertive and inquisitive. But he didn't know how to ask teachers questions without sounding belligerent. On the playground, his aggressiveness got him in fights. Hannibal ended up in special education—not because he had cognitive learning disabilities, but because his behavior made him hard to handle in a regular class.

Agin Shaheed, the pupil advocate at Hannibal's school, recognized a familiar pattern in this socially precocious, apparently slow child. The boy's street smarts got him in trouble in class, and he was typecast for failure in school—a prime candidate for joining a gang.

One day Agin saw Hannibal surrounded by a group of other boys who were "basing" each other. Basing is a children's game where kids ritually bad-mouth each other's mothers—much like the "dozens" of an older generation. The insults reach a climax until someone can't take it anymore, and this time it was Hannibal. When someone insulted his mother, he punched hard and knocked him down. Hannibal was suspended.

Agin Shaheed looked beneath Hannibal's ferocious mask and saw a boy testing his manhood in the schoolyard. From his study of African-American history, Agin knew that basing began in slave days, when children watched their parents debased by masters and sold down the river. It was a way of showing that, no matter what horrible thing was done or said, the youth was strong enough to survive and not reveal his hurt. Agin saw Hannibal, the stepson of a domineering marine, excelling at basing as a misdirected leadership skill.

He brought the boy into his room filled with African artifacts and portraits of black inventors, from ancient Egypt to contemporary America. Hannibal had a mental block about math. Agin told him that Hannibal's ancestors in Ethiopia had a tradition of mathematics. Euclid was an African mathematician who is known by his Greek name.

"I want you to remember, Hannibal, that Africans were among the first identified mathematicians in the world culture, and you need to take your place in the tradition."

Hannibal, who was dark and had a broad nose, felt bad about his appearance. But Agin showed him pictures of African princes, males like Hannibal who had African features. He also gave Hannibal a picture of Marcus

Garvey, whom the boy resembles, and Hannibal devoured an illustrated book about the early African-American leader. He began to take pride in his heritage, his identity, himself. Agin started to teach Hannibal ways to communicate with authority figures. Instead of demanding an answer, he advised, treat your teacher with respect and that is how you will be treated in return. Instead of acting like you know everything when you secretly feel afraid you don't know, show your teacher you are anxious to learn.

Hannibal began to respond. He was taken out of special education and put in a regular class. He continued to excel. The next year, he was tested and put in a class for gifted students.

Hannibal's transformation illustrates a parable by which Agin Shaheed, assuming the voice of an African storyteller, explains to his boys the intricate process of growing up. As he tells the parable, the boys' faces grow intent and their eyes widen with wonder as they enter an oral tradition going back to Africa. The parable of the caterpillar and the cocoon explains the process of human transformation to children, and goes like this:

The caterpillar, that lowly creature who is bound to earth and easily stepped on, eats a diet of moist, green leaves. Crawling to a safe place, the caterpillar spits out a silken thread and wraps itself into a cocoon. Hanging above the ground that held it in check, out of the view of the rest of creation, the caterpillar hides in the cocoon. There it goes through a marvelous change—a metamorphosis—and emerges from the cocoon as a butterfly. The brilliantly colored butterfly flutters over creation in full view of everything that held it in check, and all prize its beauty and admire its flight. The butterfly moves from flower to flower, taking for its diet the sweet nectar of creation.

The analogy Agin describes for his boys is that the caterpillar stage is elementary school, when children begin consuming the leaves of a book. Students digest rich leaves of mathematics, reading, social studies. They need moist, green leaves, rich with emotion and flexibility, not just dry, academic leaves. If they only eat wet leaves, they will develop emotionally but not academically, for their cocoon will have no structure to hold the caterpillar; the wet cocoon will fall apart and the creature will die. On the other hand, a dry cocoon, all study and no emotional expression, also kills the caterpillar, trapping him in a tomb of knowledge estranged from life. Elementary school is the caterpillar stage, junior high is the cocoon, and high school is when butterflies emerge with their personalities and fly off to college or vocational school.

"Every time you see a butterfly," Agin concludes, "I want you to remember this story. Right now, you're in elementary school. Eat all the leaves you can—read, read, read. Make sure the leaves are moist and green, that you have caring with your knowledge."

The spring of the program's third year, the rains came and there was a great migration of monarch butterflies to southern California. Agin Shaheed and his boys looked out the window and the branches of the trees were covered with golden butterflies.

In 1992, Hannibal had perfect attendance and a B average. One day on the playground, he came up to Agin and said, "I'm working on my cocoon." Hannibal's success was not a solitary one. The behavior and grades of the black youths in the program began to improve, and the school's results on standardized tests began to climb. Although the three-year experiment was not over, preliminary results gave the school district evidence that with nurturing, even the most forbidding students could make transformations toward achievement. In a similar program at the Amidon Elementary School in Washing-ton, D.C., black girls in an African-American female role-model program learned to cope with teenage pregnancy and sexual abuse, and to develop self-esteem. These programs should serve as examples to other ethnic groups and classes, including millions of white children living in single-parent homes with little or no contact with absent fathers.

As hopeful as these school and child-development programs are, their number is few in comparison to the millions of American children growing up without guidance and protection, trapped in cocoons of poverty, neglect, and abuse.

Our national development is predicated on child development, and the steps we take to help children grow, support families, engage absent parents, and improve schools will determine whether this nation takes positive steps forward—or whether we fall all the way down the stairs to Third World poverty.

All of this becomes mere rhetoric unless the economic plight of children is faced head-on by the president and Congress. In 1991, it appeared that Washington might finally wake up and address the needs of children. The National Commission on Children had confronted the stark realities facing children and their families, and hammered out a consensus strategy for action by all levels of American society, from our house to the White House.

Boiled down, the 519-page report advocated action on four fronts: child development, health, family support, and education. Child development means doing on a national scale what pilot programs like Families First are doing with children and mothers in Auburn, Washington.

Health means making sure that every child has access to preventive and comprehensive health care. In this way, children like A.J. Miller, who have catastrophic medical expenses, don't bankrupt the families they depend on. Family support means recognizing that children depend on families—however people choose to define them—and that families need child care, counseling, and support services such as those provided by the Center for Family Life in Brooklyn. Education means getting schools involved in child development and involving parents in schools, as exemplified by the Comer model in Leavenworth, Kansas.

The National Commission's report was accurately named "Beyond Rhetoric," because it provided a comprehensive, commonsense, economically feasible blueprint for action. But when the media got hold of the finely balanced report, all it saw was the red flag—a $1,000 refundable tax credit for all children through age 18. Immediately, the report was tagged as another big-spending government program and promptly dismissed. Nobody thought to ask how many thousands of dollars are being borrowed from every child's future to pay our $4 trillion debt.

Until our leaders take seriously their responsibility for protecting America's children, there is no solution to raising children and healing families except day-to-day involvement in their lives. For impoverished children bearing this nation's debt on their backs, there is no alternative but to transfer education, responsibility, and, yes, money from the older generations to the younger.

The steps we take need not be grandiose, but rather may be compared to the first steps a child takes, with plenty of room to fall, get up, and try again. The toddlers climbing on playground equipment are taking risks, and all children need basic developmental tools to climb the stair steps of life. If left to fend for themselves, children easily fall down the stairs into the hell of abuse and separation. Comprehensive family-support services are the beginnings of a railing for children to grasp as they make their way to school. There, growth resembles the magical transformations of Agin Shaheed's caterpillar turning into a butterfly—an antidote to poverty's toxic cocoon.

ADOLESCENCE

COMING OF AGE IN AMERICA

Coming of age in America is perhaps the most dangerous transition, because the handrail guiding teens through adolescence is broken or missing. Teenagers teeter on the shaky stair between childhood and adulthood, flailing against adults with one hand while reaching out to them with the other. Every generation takes risks, but this generation is plagued by high-caliber weapons, lethal drugs, and a fatal sexually transmitted disease that make the turbulent sixties look benign.

Today's teenagers lack hope. They are the first generation of Americans since the Great Depression to expect a lower standard of living than their parents. Opportunities to find a job with a future are diminishing, while the economic and social penalties for getting pregnant, dropping out of school, or breaking the law are more severe than before.

Given these conditions, it is remarkable that many at-risk adolescents manage to acquire skills, form an identity, and grow up. Their successes are too rarely reported, and raise the inevitable questions: How did these youngsters manage to transform their lives, who helped them, how much did it cost—and what lessons can be learned?

Three adolescents who made it against terrible odds provide partial answers: Cheryl is a white teenage mother from Washington State, Timothy is a battered black youth from Detroit, and Claribel is an orphaned high school student who grew up in Puerto Rico and New Jersey. All three teenagers confronted crises capable of destroying a young person, yet each received help at a crucial juncture. Their lives, with all the blemishes, mistakes, beauty, and courage of youth, provide insights not only about their personal survival, but about how adults can build a railing to support youths slipping on the stair of adolescence.

Every year, a million teenage girls get pregnant, and roughly half a million deliver babies. America has the highest teenage pregnancy rate in the industrialized world, ten times higher than Japan and three times higher than Western Europe. For poor girls, teen motherhood is an enslavement to the shackling cycle of children giving birth to children. For middle-class teenagers, it's a one-way ticket to poverty.

Cheryl was a competitive high school junior who excelled in sports and dreamed of going away to college, until she accidentally became pregnant at age sixteen. It happened in October 1988, and the chaotic events that would irrevocably change her life are as painful in their details as the basic pattern is commonplace.

Cheryl grew up in a white, middle-class Mormon family in the Pacific Northwest. Cheryl's father had little truck with blacks, but Cheryl's mother was open to people of color. When Cheryl was growing up, one of her mother's friends was a spirited black grandmother. She was raising her grandson, Kyle, who had been abandoned as a baby by his mother. Kind and playful, with a wonderful sense of humor, Kyle became Cheryl's childhood friend, until his grandmother moved away when they were in elementary school.

Several years later, Kyle and his grandmother drove

from their home in Portland, Oregon, to visit Cheryl and her family in Auburn, Washington. The two teenagers hadn't seen each other for what seemed ages—actually a year—and were bubbling with excitement to share their inner thoughts and feelings as they used to do before Kyle moved away. One moment they were watching television and lying on the recreation room floor, where Cheryl's mother had trustingly laid out two sleeping bags for them; the next moment, they were making love. It was the second time in Cheryl's young life that she engaged in sex. She had no birth-control device, but Kyle, who was fifteen, used a condom. The next day, he and his grandmother drove home to Oregon, never to return.

Cheryl's sexual initiation at age sixteen was about average for her generational group: Half of white teenage girls become sexually active between age fifteen and nineteen, and half of them use condoms for birth control. But condoms sometimes fail, as Cheryl discovered after she missed two periods.

She was shocked to learn that she was exactly two months pregnant; Kyle was, without doubt, the father. Convulsed with tears, feeling utterly alone, she didn't understand how it happened to her the second time she had sex, when other girls "did it" frequently, without protection, and never got pregnant. She agonized over whether she should terminate the pregnancy or give up her college dreams for the future. Kyle, who wanted no part of fatherhood, told her to stop hassling him and get an abortion. Cheryl's mother, who opposed abortion for religious reasons, urged Cheryl to go through with the pregnancy and put the baby up for adoption. Cheryl was terrified of telling her father that she was pregnant, and by whom. It would be bad enough that his daughter, the apple of his eye, would become a teenage mother, but for her father to have an illegitimate black grandchild was simply unthinkable.

At sixteen, Cheryl joined an increasing number of teenagers of all backgrounds who faced the pervasive nightmare of their age group—an unwanted pregnancy. Her situation reflects a complex statistical reality that belies stereotypes. First, about one-third of the girls in her age group are at risk of pregnancy. Second, minority teenagers are more likely than whites to have babies, but the percentage of white girls like Cheryl has been growing faster than all other groups. Third, the number of teenage mothers has been declining since the 1970s, but the rate of teenage mothers who marry has declined even faster. The result is that more teenage mothers become single parents living in poverty, barely able to support their babies.

As the negative consequences for teenage mothers and their babies grow more severe, the antiabortion movement has grown more vocal in pressuring young women to have their babies. If abortion ever becomes illegal in America, some 400,000 fetuses now aborted each year could be born to teenage mothers who do not want them and probably aren't mature enough to raise them.

For teens like Cheryl who choose to have their babies, the reward is almost certain stigmatization and poverty. The shameful bigotry against an innocent child, whose only "crime" is having parents of different races, is only a part of it. The most serious form of discrimination against teenage mothers and their babies is not racial but economic. America is an equal-opportunity discriminator against single-parent families, half of whom are condemned to live in poverty. If an adolescent mother—half girl and half woman—hasn't developed the ability to support herself emotionally and practically, if her boyfriend doesn't offer any real support, and if her parents disapprove and reject her, having a baby becomes a calamity.

Rather than face the humiliation of going through pregnancy in her hometown, Cheryl opted to move to another city. Through her family's connections in the Mormon church, a couple in Olympia, Washington, heard of her plight, supported her decision to have her baby, and agreed to take her in for the duration of her pregnancy. The day she arrived, unpacked her suitcase in a cheerless bedroom, and enrolled in a new high school was her seventeenth birthday. During lunch hour at school, she sat on the stairs and cried, oblivious to gawkers.

"Today is my second day at the Walkers' house," she wrote in her diary. "They are very nice, but I know the next five months are probably going to be the hardest in my life. Telling my dad and seeing the disappointment and hurt on his face was probably the hardest part of being pregnant so far. My mom came up and visited me today. I hate saying good-bye, 'cause I know the minute she drives off I'll be alone."

The high school had no special classes or counseling for teenagers in Cheryl's position, and her isolation grew so severe that she could barely concentrate on her studies. Students whispered behind her back that she was a "slut," while teachers treated her like a delinquent. After a month of this hell, she heard about a special program at another high school that helped pregnant teens learn about their babies and make it to graduation. She transferred to Olympia High School and enrolled in the Teenage Parenting Program, TAP, along with twenty other teenage mothers.

In order to help pregnant teens become viable mothers, the state of Washington has twenty-nine school-based programs like TAP. The program costs about $2,000 per mother and baby. Only 1,400 of the state's 8,500 eligible teen mothers are enrolled, however. Those who drop out have a hard time supporting themselves, and inevitably put a burden on the state for social services.

The cost imposed on American society when young women and men drop out of school is astronomical. "Each year's class of dropouts costs the nation approximately $260 billion in lost earnings and forgone taxes over their lifetimes," the National Commission of Children reported in 1991. "More than $20 billion per year is spent at the federal level alone for Aid to Families with Dependent Children, Medicaid, and food stamps for families begun by a birth as a teenager."

Although Cheryl herself had been raised in a relatively stable home, most of her colleagues had been victims of sexual assaults during childhood. A 1992 study of pregnant teens in Washington State found that two-thirds of teenage mothers had prior histories of sexual abuse. Chillingly, the study concluded that abused women were also more likely to abuse their children, a pattern that condemns generation after generation.

TAP supported its mothers through the crises of pregnancy. A teacher, counselor, and nurse teamed up to provide pregnancy and parenting classes, as well as on-site child care while the mothers were in class. The program was headed by Barbara Crump, a no-nonsense teacher who worked hard to gain the girls' trust, then taught them how to set goals, make decisions, solve problems— the practical skills of living that many had never learned at home.

"If you can deal with crises in adolescence, these techniques will help you later on in your twenties, thirties, forties, and fifties," Barbara Crump said. As their babies grew, she taught mothers, week by week, about the ages and stages of development. Because child abuse often results from parents having unreasonable expectations of their babies, knowing their limitations helps prevent abuse.

Cheryl took a full class schedule in addition to TAP. She no longer felt alone, that her life was over. She became motivated to move forward in a progression that, she hoped, would lead to the accomplishment of her dreams. Barbara helped Cheryl deal with the paralyzing fear of her father's anger and encouraged her to make her own choices.

"I felt the baby move today for the first time," she wrote in her diary. Although she did not judge other girls in worse circumstances who chose to terminate their pregnancies, she wrote: "I thank myself every day that I did not have an abortion. I know being pregnant has hurt a lot of people, including me, but it's almost over and everything can go back to normal."

A week before delivery, Cheryl gathered the courage to confront her father. They sat across from each other on sawhorses in his garage. She told him the baby's father was black and that she had decided to keep the child. Angrily, he told her not to bring a black baby home. After he stomped out, Cheryl dissolved into tears, but her mother put her foot down: Her grandchild was staying.

The baby, a girl, was born in Olympia at 10:02 P.M. on July 20, 1989.* Cheryl's mother was with her in the delivery room. Her father sat silently in the waiting room for twelve hours; the moment the baby's cry was heard, he stood up and walked out. The baby had black hair and skin the color of creamed coffee, and Cheryl named her Kayla. Cheryl paid for the delivery herself, emptying her bank account of $1,500 she had earned and saved for college.

---

* Kayla was born two weeks before A. J. Miller was born, and a month before Kenya Williams' first crack-exposed baby died.

The next day she confided to her diary that any doubts about keeping Kayla had vanished at 10:02 P.M., the "happiest moment" of her life. But she worried whether her father would ever come to accept, much less love, his granddaughter.

Cheryl brought Kayla home to a basement room in her parents' house, and for two weeks she didn't come out for fear of triggering her father's ire. As luck would have it, a group of relatives who came to visit swept Kayla into their arms and welcomed her into the bosom of the family. Cheryl saw her father jealously watching them hugging his grandchild. After three weeks, he picked Kayla up for the first time. Soon, the grandfather and granddaughter became inseparable.

Cheryl transferred back to Auburn High School for her senior year, but there was no teen mother program and no on-site baby-sitting. "We have a place for *people like you* to go," she was told. Cheryl refused to be put in an alternative high school, and she endured the loneliness of being the only graduating senior with a child. Her mother took care of Kayla during school hours; Cheryl did all the rest. Taking parenting classes, washing Kayla's diapers (she couldn't afford disposable ones), working part-time to pay her parents rent, and studying between feedings, she managed to graduate with a 3.44 average—just shy of honors.

While her friends went off to college, Cheryl contemplated a bleak future dependent on welfare. She received no child support from Kyle. Once, she drove down to Portland, hoping to get Kyle involved with his daughter, but he preferred to smoke dope with his friends, and she left after forty-five minutes. She has not seen him again.

Kyle's lack of responsibility is typical; more than 80 percent of the fathers of such babies do not pay child support. Their lack of involvement is caused by many factors—immaturity, inability to find a job to support the baby, callous disregard—but the consequences for fatherless children are devastating.

Cheryl's luck improved when she learned of a new program designed especially for babies and single mothers that was starting up in Auburn. Families First, the same comprehensive child-development program that Peg Mazen directed, challenged Cheryl to set reasonable goals and work toward achieving them. Her first goal was to move out of her parents' house into her own apartment so she could have a more independent relationship and establish her own family. Her long-term goal was to graduate from college.

The problems facing single mothers living on welfare are not those highlighted by stereotypes of the welfare madonna. Cheryl received $428 a month in public assistance. The lowest rents in her community were $300 a month for a studio in a bad neighborhood, and day care cost $400 a month. If she worked, most of the earnings would be deducted from her welfare check and she'd risk losing Medicaid for Kayla. She couldn't afford child care to attend college. Instead of helping Cheryl become self-sufficient, welfare trapped her and Kayla in poverty.

Families First encouraged her to apply for Section 8 federal housing assistance and helped her locate a two-bedroom apartment. Instead of being isolated in a housing project for the poor, Cheryl received a rent subsidy that reduced her rent from $525 to $70 a month, and she lived in a modern private development. Families First helped her acquire simple home furnishings, insisting that she pay for half of everything. For the first time, Kayla got regular medical checkups that focused on prevention.

At age one, Kayla entered Family First's child-care program a bit delayed in development. She soon made rapid strides in talking, walking, and playing with other children, becoming advanced for her age. Cheryl enrolled in community college, working toward a two-year degree as a paralegal, but she soon decided that she wanted a four-year college degree. Her goal now is to become a probation counselor or a counselor with teen parents, and to start her own TAP program in Auburn. She is active on the governing council of the Families First program and is the youngest member on the board of trustees for the Children's Home Society. She has begun dating, and is looking for a responsible husband who will accept Kayla. She dreams of having a family like her parents, who are celebrating their twenty-fifth wedding anniversary.

Families First spends about $15,000 a year helping a family like Cheryl's stay independent and healthy while mother and child go to their respective schools. The program costs less than the minimum $20,000 a year that would be spent providing foster care to a teen and her baby, and potentially saves thousands of dollars in extra medical care, rehabilitation, and special education. In two years Cheryl is expected to graduate and will begin to support her family by her work, paying taxes to help others.

"Families First helped me become independent—that's the best thing," Cheryl told me, flushing with pride. "I feel I'm accomplishing something myself. If there were more programs like these, there would be fewer dependent people."

Cheryl sometimes regrets losing her childhood, but she has developed self-assurance by raising her baby. The transformation from adolescence to adulthood was accomplished by hard work and the help of others. Their lasting gift was to make Cheryl self-reliant, without feeling alone and isolated, within a community of caring.

*   *   *

Perhaps the most damaged group of American teenagers
are boys growing up without fathers. They suffer not only
physical and mental deprivation, but also grow up without older men to guide them. Every year, nearly 6,000
young males are murdered in America, many of them at
the hands of other teenagers. Black, Latino, and poor
white teenage boys live in combat conditions unknown to
civilians since the Civil War.

Coming of age in the projects of Boyle Heights, a
Latino barrio of Los Angeles, is a baptism of gunfire and
blood for fatherless adolescent boys from decimated families. Some of these boys will seek kinship in gangs.
Father Gregory Boyle of the Dolores Mission Church has
buried twenty-six kids, most of them boys who needed
fathers to guide them through adolescence. He tells of
Mario Sugar Bear from Quatro Flats, a huge teenager
with a volatile temper—especially when he became
drunk. In the summer of '91, Mario's younger brother Fat
Rat was shot in the leg by a rival gang. After doctors told
Father Boyle that Fat Rat was going to make it, he began
searching for Sugar Bear, who was bound by the gang
code to take revenge for the shooting. All night Father
Boyle searched, and finally he found Sugar Bear alone,
leaning against a lamppost. Father Boyle told him his
brother was going to be fine.

"Do you know how angry I am?" Sugar Bear cried. He
had gone to all his homeys—friends who shared the
street battle for identity in a tough neighborhood—but
no one would give him a gun. He went to nearby factory
yards in the predawn light and sat by himself. "I did
something I never did before," he told the priest. "I
started to pray." Sugar Bear began to cry, telling the
father about a voice deep inside him that told him,

109

"Don't do it." He cried all the more, confessing, "I've never listened to that voice before."

From the moment he heard that voice, Sugar Bear decided he was no longer going to play the game of gang violence; he started to work at the parish, building a child-care center for the children. He worked six months, staying clean and separating himself from the gang. One day, he joked with the priest: "When I die, I want you to do my funeral and play that old Supremes song, 'Someday We'll Be Together.'" The next day, another gang drove by to retaliate for a skirmish and mistook Sugar Bear for a rival gang member. They shot him dead and careened away in their car. He was nineteen.

Father Boyle, an outspoken Jesuit priest with a graying beard and wire-rimmed glasses, has been pastor at the Dolores Mission Church in Boyle Heights—no family relation—for six years. The neighborhood is almost wholly Latino, with second-generation Chicanos, immigrants from Mexico and Central America. Slums in Los Angeles don't look like the urban ghettos of the South Bronx; the colors are brighter and there are palm trees, but within the crowded housing projects, drugs and violence are endemic, and families are embattled.

Father Boyle scoffs at those who believe that more police and bigger prisons can stop the violence. Gang violence is not ultimately a legal issue but an economic one, he believes, because society can't just say no to gangs and will them away. The real problem is that single mothers can't feed their kids, can't pay the rent, can't afford the luxury of going to parenting classes. Fatherless boys who lack guidance to become men join gangs in a desperate attempt to raise each other to manhood.

No one in Los Angeles will voluntarily hire Father Boyle's boys, so he begs and borrows to pay businesses to hire them. He has forty-seven kids working in construction, maintenance, gardening, and warehouse crews, and every Friday the father goes to all the workplaces and gives the employers money to pay the boys' salaries.

"The closest thing to a single solution is a job," Father Boyle told me in late April 1992. "It's the only thing I know that quiets the bullets. Jobs give a sense of pride and dignity, a reason to get up in the morning. If you cannot imagine a future for yourself, you don't care if you inflict harm—or are in harm's way. A job can lift a kid out of despair."

Two days after our conversation, a jury acquitted four Los Angeles police officers who'd been videotaped savagely beating motorist Rodney King. Los Angeles began to burn. As the plumes of smoke rose, gang members warned Father Boyle that the violence was coming to his neighborhood. He took to the streets with a simple message: "Here is what I've done for you, and here is what I am going to ask of you." Father Boyle passed a warehouse that was just beginning to be looted. He recognized many faces of people he had helped, and his presence was enough to persuade them to leave. The line broke up and the warehouse was not looted. As L.A. was engulfed by the worst civil disturbance in modern America, Boyle Heights was spared.

"Part of the reason is that we have programs that take the edge off," Father Boyle explained to the *Los Angeles Times*. "We also have a good sense of community here."

Talk of rebuilding L.A. in the aftermath of the riots focused on buildings, not families. It was about blaming the violence on race and poverty, not acknowledging the importance of absent fathers. A 1988 study of fifty-seven neighborhoods across the country revealed that children of all races and backgrounds who grow up without fathers are more likely to commit violent crimes, but this foot-note was ignored.

While the violence in L.A. was spreading to other poor, disenfranchised ghettos across America, the Sunset Park community of Brooklyn was quiet. This was not because there was no social injustice, but largely because young people in Sunset Park were growing up with hope in a community that was involved with their problems. The process of helping young people began much earlier, in the late 1970s, when Sisters Mary Paul and Geraldine won back the territory from gangs with a unique combi-nation of toughness and love.

Sunset Park, which is only one mile wide and two and a half miles long, is as compact as Los Angeles is sprawling. From a hill in the park from which the neighborhood gets its name, one can see the Statue of Liberty. Most of the residents are immigrants—not the European immigrants who passed through Ellis Island, but new immigrants from Latin America and the Caribbean. Before the Center for Family Life moved in, Sunset Park was heir to many of the divisions that tore apart American cities, and young people were both victims and victimizers.

The nuns' strategy to attract teenagers was simple: Host a dance. But this posed a problem, because gangs wanted to control the dance on their turf, spray-painting graffiti on buildings and threatening children. The nuns set down basic rules: No colors. Everyone is invited. No one is excluded.

Teens were drawn to participate, because at that time, 1979, there were no dances in the neighborhood and the gangs ruled the streets. The nuns hosted the first dances in the barrio, one a month. With the cooperation of a Lutheran minister who ran his youth mission out of a van, they faced innumerable challenges to their authority, but moved from turf to turf to open up programs for the community of 100,000 people.

The nuns interpreted gang phenomena as the values and structures that teenagers held on to as they grew up in a dangerous environment: Gangs valued loyalty, following rules, and cohesiveness; gang colors were a kind of uniform of belonging, like the nuns' blue habits. The sisters spent a lot of time developing trust, and then they began to substitute values and alternative structures. In the after-school programs involving 500 children, they created groups based on camp models, with kids working step-by-step to become counselors in training, assistant counselors, and group leaders. Each group had a name, like the Hot Tootsies, and a group identity. The older adolescents had roles of responsibility and honor, leading the younger children in activities. A few adults, including a professional dancer from the Martha Graham company with a lot of skills to give away, made the groups' activities—plays, music, dance, art shows—the envy of gangs.

It soon became more impressive, exciting, and involving for a teen to be a group leader than a gang leader, and there were waiting lists for people to join. When problems of violence and authority inevitably arose, they weren't swept under the rug, but faced squarely by bringing everyone involved into group sessions, including teens' families. A charismatic male recreation director became a respected figure whom boys looked up to for fatherly advice; he could talk tough, yet he showed them manly ways to handle disputes without resorting to violence.

The shift from a gang model to a counselor model took commitment to accomplish, but over thirteen years the Center for Family Life has slowly transformed Sunset Park from a neighborhood divided by gangs into a community united behind families. Children grow up in the program; moving from Teddy Bears to teenage group leaders, they develop a sense of self by being committed beyond themselves. They in turn try to pass their experience on to younger children. As one Sunset Park father says, "A tree grows straight if it has straight people around it."

For Timothy of Detroit, who grew up with an alcoholic father and a mother who neglected him at an early age, there was no Center for Family Life to help him through the traumas of childhood and adolescence. Timothy's first memory was standing over the kitchen stove, trying to get warmed by the gas flame. He was only four years old when his mother left him for a little while one day in the care of his five-year-old sister, Regina. She said she was coming back, but the hours dragged on. The unheated house, in an impoverished ghetto of Detroit known as the Black Bottom, was so cold that water froze in the bathroom. The only warm room was in the kitchen, where the gas stove was lit.

Timothy and Regina stood side by side on the same chair, reaching toward the dancing flames. She wore a white dress that flared out on the side. Her hair was in braids. The chair wobbled. Suddenly, Timothy saw flames climb her skirt. She flapped her arms to put them out, but only fanned them higher, waving angel wings of fire. Regina was screaming but Timothy was too confused to know what to do. He watched the white polyester material melt on his sister's body.

Dropping to the ground, Timothy rolled Regina over the floor, finally managing to put out the flames. Patches of her burned skin came off on the linoleum. With all his might, he dragged her body upstairs and lifted her into bed. She was still breathing. Maybe if Regina slept, her four-year-old brother thought, she would wake up and be all right. Waiting for his parents to come home, Timothy remembers hearing someone banging on the front door and the loud voice of a man demanding to be let in. But Regina was naked and Timothy was ashamed to let a stranger see her, so he kept the door locked until the banging stopped. It was a doctor, he later learned, but he was too late to help Regina, who died soon after.

The shock to Timothy was beyond the ability of his grief-stricken parents to overcome. They never asked him to talk with them about his feelings following the tragedy. For years he lived as a pariah in the family, hounded by his father, who drunkenly raged: "You killed my daughter!" Afterward, his father would sometimes apologize and say, "You be my number one boy." Timothy was deeply confused by these vacillations: In his search for love and approval from his father, he became even more accident-prone. His father moved out and visited infrequently. Once, when his father was leaving, Timothy ran after him into the street and was grazed by a truck, surviving miraculously with a superficial head injury.

In school, he was embarrassed to find his father hanging around the fence drunk, his trousers stained with urine. Timothy's mother took up with another man, who was jealous of her attention to her sons. When this angry stepfather moved in, Timothy moved out at thirteen, sleeping on couches in relatives' homes and with friends. Timothy's older brothers were not good examples, and the neighborhood recreation center was a dangerous place. Timothy was playing pool there one day when he heard someone shout, "Freeze!" With his back to the voice, he continued to play, and a bullet slammed into his thigh. Timothy was rushed to the hospital and never saw his assailant. Later, he learned it was his older brother who had fired the bullet that accidentally struck him.

Timothy, who was six during Detroit's 1967 riots, grew up watching the city slowly burn, house by house, neighborhood by neighborhood, year after year until a wilderness of weeds sprouted in the Black Bottom where he struggled to survive. The carnage engulfing Timothy's childhood left him scarred but miraculously alive, as one by one the people around him fell: His uncle was shot twice in the head, two of his older brothers were sent to prison, his father was jailed for vagrancy, and his friends were murdered or died in car wrecks.

At fifteen, he began messing around with a neighborhood girl of fourteen, who was already a mother. He wasn't trying to make a baby, didn't even know what he was doing, just experimenting. The girl became pregnant and told Timothy that he was the father, but he merely laughed with disbelief. He said he was no fool to be tricked by a girl into assuming some other man's responsibility. He stopped seeing her, and after she delivered a baby boy, Timothy felt no connection.

Timothy's life took him down the by-now familiar, shadowy paths of the Black Bottom. There was the excitement of living on his own, the rush of drugs and gangs and women and fights, interspersed with moments of absolute fear and loneliness, with no one to turn to— no father, elder brother, friend, or mentor that he could trust. And even though he was naturally bright, he could see no way out of his downward slide, as Detroit's inner-city neighborhoods of shade trees and blue-collar homes began looking less like the automobile capital of America and more like a blitzed baghdad that suffered aerial bombing from above and social breakdown within. Timothy learned how to survive in a chaotic environment, and his development from infancy to childhood to adolescence followed a reverse path from the normal development of children.

A year or two after breaking off with the teenage mother, Timothy saw a little boy who reminded him of himself as a toddler. He asked his old girlfriend who the child's father was. "You are." Timothy was shocked. Then a door opened inside him and he saw this boy as his mirror image, bound to him by flesh and blood, his first son. With a sinking heart, he knew he had no means of supporting or sheltering this baby, whose mother was too young and poor to raise him. He looked into his son's eyes and saw him entering the tunnel of horror Timothy had been caught in since his sister had burned to death, his father had abandoned him, his mother had neglected him, and his brother had shot him. Now, hardly more than a child himself, he resolved one day to take care of his son, to become the father he had always wanted.

Timothy's horrific childhood and adolescence, which he described to me during an interview ten years later, was so hopeless that it was hard to believe that anyone could ever recover from the traumas he endured. But when I met Timothy in 1991, he was enrolled in a job-training program at Focus: HOPE, a Detroit civil rights organization that was literally retooling lives in a twenty-three-acre complex of schools and machine shops built in the shells of abandoned factories. Timothy was learning a trade to support himself and his family, and he was raising his firstborn son, who was now a teenager.

Conditions have grown worse—not better—for adolescents growing up in the nineties. No longer are they just fatherless; an epidemic of addiction has also robbed many of their mothers. A generation is coming of age without either parent to nurture or support them, in burned-out neighborhoods where virtually all sense of community has been extinguished.

A few miles from Timothy, a college-educated African-American mother is determined not to give up on throwaway kids. Erica Wright stayed in her gutted West Side neighborhood of Detroit long after most middle-class families fled to the suburbs. Sixteen years ago she began noticing children jealously hanging around the edge of the softball diamond where her son's little league team played, a ragtag group of kids without parents to pay the fees, buy the uniforms, and cheer them on. She organized an alternative softball league that was free for all children to join, so long as they helped her cut the weeds from the trashed schoolyard where she unearthed an abandoned baseball diamond. Wright's field of dreams is one block from a gutted house where an elderly lady was burned to death in a fire set by crackheads seeking to rob her. Although far from the wheat farms of Kansas, it is filled with the spirit of hope.

The baseball diamond became the center of an informal sports organization called the West Side Cultural and Athletic Club. Wright hosts a summer Olympics for street kids, pitting dozens of the neighborhood's fastest runners in a footrace against despair. The club is located in a house that Wright bought from a fleeing neighbor for $50; it boasts no exercise equipment, no library—only a basement room with a broken table and a lamp without the shade.

When I visited one wintry night, the teenagers were so suspicious of a white journalist coming into their neighborhood after dark that they refused to let me take notes or record their voices on a tape recorder, so I have no record of their words or names. But the message they gave me, like marooned sailors putting a message in a bottle with little hope of anyone ever reading it, was one of utter abandonment—not only by their parents, but by society at large. They believed that AIDS and crack were plagues that white America had knowingly conspired to lay waste their neighborhood and wipe them out. As I listened in the darkened room, their faces limned by the dim bulb took on a timeless quality of human suffering and alienation. Gradually their anger spent itself, giving way first to hurt, then to youthful enthusiasm.

They took me on a midnight tour of a neighborhood plagued by frequent power outages, of derelict streets looming beneath darkened streetlights. Their steaming breaths rose in ghostly clouds in the frosty air, and their voices, cracking with adolescence, bubbled with excitement as they talked of their plans to rehab the clubhouse, to organize more games and teams. They showed me the shimmering tracks where the summer Olympics races drew hundreds of participants; they told me about winners past, about their dreams of winning the footrace. Anyone hearing their dreams would recognize the American dream of kids hoping to grow up to be stars— yet they came from homes where they were ignored; where desperate mothers traded their boys' new basketball shoes, bought with savings from bagging groceries, for a hit of crack; where teenagers had no hope of escaping, no matter how fast they ran or how many home runs they hit, from the grinding gears of poverty in rusting Motown.

The sights were typical of such neighborhoods in aging American cities—a boarded-up crack house riddled with bullets, a hotel where prostitutes turned tricks, markets run by immigrants from the Middle East and Asia. Inside one Iraqi-American grocery, a yellowing newspaper clipping was posted; the photo showed Erica being hugged by First Lady Barbara Bush. Erica said she'd been invited to meet Mrs. Bush as an example of what people could do for themselves, but the encounter didn't lead to her youth program being declared an official Point of Light; no funding dropped out of the sky for her kids; it just ended up as a photo opportunity for the White House, and Erica felt used. Erica was equally fed up with journalists—people like me—who came in and asked personal questions, admiring her good works, and then left. All the publicity, she said, added up to nothing for her kids.

She needed $13,000 to get the playground fixed, a van to transport some of the 230 seniors in her Adopt-a-Grandparent program, and money to turn an abandoned warehouse into a decent recreation center for her 400 kids. But she couldn't even convince the city schools to cut the weeds so they could use the baseball diamond. Her voice, weary after years of work, was edged with bitterness and despair.

Out of her frustration comes another lesson: If grassroots programs are prone to wither and die, it's because they need to be watered and fertilized by sources of funding outside the depleted neighborhoods where they are struggling to survive.

The statistical odds for Erica's kids to make it out alive are frightening. Detroit often leads the nation in homicides, the number one cause of death for black teenagers, and black teens are nine times more likely to be murdered than white teens. On any given day in America, one out of twelve black males in his twenties is in prison or jail. More African-American youths are serving time or are on parole than are currently enrolled in college.

It is clear that children coming of age in neighborhoods like Detroit's West Side or L.A.'s Boyle Heights are doomed to harm themselves or others unless older men and women are there to help them make it. Yet no matter how successful these grass-roots programs are, the

Erica Wrights of America's neighborhoods cannot do it alone. Institutional supports are necessary to help teens, and the best place to build them is in the public schools.

Perhaps the most promising effort to build a railing of social services into high schools is being made by the state of New Jersey. In the mid-1980s, the Garden State shocked America with headlines of teenage suicide pacts in suburban schools. One hundred fifteen teenagers took their lives in one year (1984), eerily equaling the number who were victims of homicide. More than 20,000 cases of child abuse and neglect were confirmed annually; nearly 10,000 teens were classified as emotionally disturbed; each year, 10,000 teenage mothers gave birth, 80 percent of them unmarried. This litany reflects trends of abuse, neglect, suicide, pregnancy, and violence that teenagers suffered across America, but New Jersey decided to take action.

Ed Tetelman, a poverty lawyer turned social service administrator, believed that the schools should not only be teaching—they should be supporting teenagers grappling with suicide, domestic violence, gangs, and abuse. Ed saw a structural flaw in the way states divided responsibilities for dealing with teens' needs. The schools were given the job of educating teenagers and social services were given the responsibility of helping families in need; mental health, on the other hand, was neglected. Many children fell through the cracks between institutions. They dropped out of school and dropped into the welfare roles, never receiving help to deal with adolescent crises that, once resolved, would enable them to graduate and enter society productively.

Ed's idea was simple: Use the schools as a base to provide basic social services—health care, family counseling, drug education, employment, tutorial, and recreation—to teenagers at risk. In 1988, the New Jersey Department of Social Services established the School-Based Youth Services Program for twenty-nine agencies in twenty-one counties throughout the state.

"We put services where the kids are," Ed says. The core services are mental health and family counseling, primary preventive health services, employment services, and substance-abuse counseling. It doesn't matter if the teenager comes from a poor family or if his father is a millionaire. If help is needed, it is provided.

In New Brunswick, New Jersey, Superintendent of Schools Dr. Ronald F. Larkin endorses the School-Based program because test scores are higher, attendance is up, discipline problems and dropout rates are declining. "I don't know how we could run a high school without School-Based," he says, "It's the wave of the future."

In Dover, New Jersey, the School-Based program called Tiger RAP (Tiger is the school mascot and RAP stands for Reach-Out Assistance Program) was tested to its limits by the plight of a Puerto Rican teenager and her three young siblings. The successful intervention by the program's director, Linda Seeley, and her committed staff shows that even in the most extreme circumstances, a young person can assume adult responsibility with practical support and counseling.

This is the story of a child-woman whose young life was split between two worlds and whose family was consumed by domestic violence. Claribel spent about half her youth in her mother's hometown of Aguada, Puerto Rico. The other half was spent in Dover, New Jersey, a fading industrial town with a rising Latino population and located an hour from Newark.

Claribel was seventeen years old when her stepfather

shot her mother to death and then committed suicide in front of her baby brother. The killings occurred in Aguada, and Claribel was left to raise three younger siblings alone, poor and homeless. She feared they would be trapped in misery if they remained in the small town. Still in mourning, she brought her destitute siblings and grandmother to Dover, New Jersey, hoping to find a better life in the town where she'd spent much of her childhood. They moved in with her aunt in public housing, but were reported to be living there without permission, and evicted. A month after their mother was slain, they were homeless on the streets of Dover.

In September 1989, Kelly Gleason, a bilingual counselor at the Tiger RAP program, received an emergency call regarding a Puerto Rican girl who had enrolled at Dover High: "Stepfather killed her mother. Four siblings homeless . . . living in motel. Four-year-old suffering trauma from witnessing his father killing his mother."

Kelly hung up in shock. She had helped teens going through predictable crises, but didn't know if she could cope with so many grave problems. She sent a note asking Claribel to come to her office in a trailer behind the high school.

It was a sunny Friday afternoon about 3 P.M. when Claribel arrived with her six-year-old sister, Manuela. With long black hair falling over crescent-shaped eyes that were ringed from lack of sleep, Claribel was hauntingly beautiful but disoriented. Manuela was pale and thin, like a war refugee from Central America. Kelly, a social worker who had studied psychology, noted clinical signs of posttraumatic stress syndrome.

Claribel listened intently while Kelly described the program and invited her to attend weekly counseling sessions. Then Kelly asked Claribel to talk about herself. It was the first time that anyone had really listened, and Claribel felt the terrible weight that she carried melt into tears.

The violence began long before, in Puerto Rico, where Claribel's first memory was her natural father throwing her mother down the stairs. It continued after her mother divorced him and brought Claribel and her brother Jorge to New Jersey, where she married again. Sadly, the new husband proved to be even more brutal and selfish. He fathered two children, Manuela and Manny, but neglected Claribel and Jorge. Claribel attended grade school in New Jersey, then her stepfather took the family back to Puerto Rico, where he was offered a good job. But he continued beating her mother and neglecting the children. As a teenager, Claribel tried to protect her battered mother but couldn't.

In August 1989, her mother attempted one last time to leave her husband. The night before moving out with her children, she and Claribel stayed up late, planning and laughing. Claribel fell asleep in her mother's bed, dreaming of her new life. Early next morning, Claribel left her sleeping mother, tiptoed out of the bedroom, and walked to school. She would always regret not awakening her mother and kissing her good-bye.

That same morning, Claribel's stepfather, who had been drinking, visited Manuela in her first-grade class. "Mommy and Daddy are leaving," he said. Manuela was confused because she thought she was going with her mother. Frightened, she asked where her parents were going, but her father only looked at her sadly and said it was far away.

Four-year-old Manny was at home when his raging-drunk father burst into the bedroom. He did not understand why his father leapt upon his mother and started beating her up. But by all accounts, the attack was premeditated: Insanely jealous that his wife was leaving him, he was determined not to let her go, even if it meant killing her.

"Don't hurt Mommy!" Manny cried.

His father smashed her head against the bedpost, breaking her nose, and ripped her face open—a gash appeared above her eye socket. She screamed, trying to get away from him. He pulled her back, leaving streaks of blood on the door, threw her on the bed, and shot her several times in the chest. As she slid to the floor, he turned the pistol on himself; it misfired, tearing open his throat and wounding, but not killing, him.

Hearing shots, neighbors rushed to the house and tried to disarm him. Despite his bleeding wound, he broke away and staggered back to the bedroom. Reloading all six chambers, he fired point-blank into his wife's heart. Finally, sure she was dead and could never betray his demented love, he killed himself.

Claribel was called out of school and knew without being told that something had happened to her mother. They took her to her grandmother's house, where Jorge cried, "They killed Mommy!" Claribel assumed the terrible task of telling her little sister, Manuela, that Mommy and Daddy were gone forever. Then they brought Manny to her. Shaking, his hair matted and his clothing stiff with dried blood, he stared at Claribel with frantic eyes. He had seen everything. He couldn't speak, couldn't utter a cry.

They laid her mother's body out in their home, and Claribel made a pledge to her that she would take care of Jorge, Manuela, and Manny, no matter what. She also pledged that she would finish high school so she wouldn't have to depend financially on anyone, especially an abusive husband. Three days after arriving in New Jersey with her siblings and grandmother, Claribel registered at Dover High.

In her first session with Kelly, Claribel was so wrought up that she was unable to utter her dead stepfather's name. She didn't know if therapy would help, but she agreed to return for a second session. Before she left, Kelly gave Claribel four T-shirts emblazoned with Tiger RAP to bring home to her threadbare family. Claribel soon began to come regularly, walking three miles to Dover High, then walking home to take care of her three siblings.

Kelly also began to see Manny at the nearby Head Start center. His frightened eyes looked disturbed, and his behavior alternated between hyperactivity and depression. Manny was obsessed with memories of the murder and awoke from nightmares, crying out: "Don't hurt Mommy!" In the first session, he fashioned a gun out of clay and pointed it at Kelly. Sometimes he would bang his head on the wall, or talk to his dead father in Spanish.

She sought a child psychiatrist for him, but no Spanish-speaking therapist was available, and Manny was too traumatized to learn English. So Kelly, who is bilingual, devised her own form of play therapy, talking with Manny in Spanish and helping him express his feelings nonverbally by drawing pictures.

Claribel needed immediate assistance to find a place to live, food, and a source of income. Her grandmother, who had legal custody of the children, spoke no English and didn't know how to budget their limited resources, so they were chronically destitute. They had found temporary shelter at the Skytop Motel, a low-rent, roach-infested dive that had been turned into a homeless shelter. Another counselor at Tiger RAP, Kathy Flarety, helped Claribel find a two-bedroom unit in a four-family house. On $200, they furnished the place, and a furniture-store owner donated his best beds for the children.

Nuns provided winter clothing. School-Based was not only helping Claribel, it was providing a way for the people of Dover to help.

Working part-time, caring for her siblings, studying, walking to school, applying for guardian status, Claribel began to raise her young siblings as a surrogate mother. The turning point came when Manny, who was sucking his thumb, unconsciously called her "Mommy." Claribel was held together during this difficult period by the counseling sessions she had with Kelly three times a week. They offered her a protected time to grieve for her mother's death—and for the death of her own innocence and youth.

Every gain was matched by setbacks. When she finally received $5,000 in survivor's benefits, welfare was cut off. Kelly tried to prevent the welfare cutoff, but there was nothing she could do. The federal government, as a matter of policy, forced Claribel to spend down to the poverty level and become a pauper again before qualifying for assistance. Worse, survivor's benefits disqualified Claribel from receiving welfare, Medicaid, or child care. Only Manny got Medicaid because he was classified as mentally disturbed. Claribel was a single "parent" denied a single parent's benefits. Without the School-Based program, Claribel would have been totally destitute.

In May 1990, Claribel turned eighteen. She was now legally able to assume formal guardianship of her three siblings. Tiger RAP helped her fill out the papers and she became officially responsible for her family. Kathy Flarety also helped Claribel look for jobs and apply to college. The young woman sometimes wanted everything to be done for her, but Kathy insisted that Claribel make the calls on her own. The combination of tenderness and tough love led to difficult moments, but Claribel showed her appreciation by sending a postcard: "Kathy, I'll never forget all the things you did for me. Don't give up on me."

With their support and her own sheer perseverance, Claribel managed to attend class enough days to graduate from Dover High. It was a considerable achievement for this eighteen-year-old surrogate mother to walk up the aisle and receive her diploma.

During a trip to Dover in late 1991, I visited Claribel's modest, two-bedroom apartment. Her home was clean and freshly swept, full of memories and dreams. Fading red armchairs protected by cracked vinyl covers face a bookcase lined with framed school photos of the kids. Proudly displayed are certificates to Manuela "for outstanding effort" and to Manny, "Student of the Month" at a special-education center. Claribel shyly admits she won a finalist trophy in a "Miss Hispanic" beauty contest, but dropped out because she found it artificial. At twenty, she is a vibrant Latina whose beauty radiates from within.

Manny is still disruptive in class and sometimes gets placed in detention. He now receives psychiatric therapy paid by Medicaid, but no one else in the family has health insurance. Claribel receives $900 a month in survivor's benefits, food stamps, and Supplemental Security Income (SSI) for the kids. The family subsists far below the official U.S. poverty line. Even after receiving benefits, Claribel's siblings are among the 13 million American kids who are poor. She can't afford a car and has to walk or take public transportation everywhere. She wants to move to a roomier, safer home away from New Jersey's heavily trafficked Route 15. Her dreams are modest: to have some time for herself, to live a normal life like other people, to see her brothers and sister grow up healthy, to go dancing once in a while. Her future beckons: She has been admitted to Morris County Community College.

"I can't wait to start school," she says excitedly, hoping

to become a social worker like the women who helped her. Before enrolling, she works afternoons at the child-care center that Manny and Manuela attend, giving them special attention. She is dating a twenty-five-year-old carpet installer who doesn't drink or take drugs and is good with the children. She is still getting counseling from Kelly Gleason, to prevent the cycle of physical abuse from repeating in her family.

On Claribel's wooden desk sits her only surviving photograph of herself and her mother. In the framed snapshot, Claribel is wearing a white lace dress for *la quincena*, her fifteenth birthday, and her mother is standing behind with her arms around her. Claribel says her mother's spirit sometimes comes to her at night. In one crucial dream, her mother bent over the beds where Manny, Manuela, and Jorge were sleeping and tenderly brushed their cheeks, finally at peace.

Tiger RAP is authorized to help Claribel's family as long as any one of the children is in school. She calls the program her guardian angel. On average, the School-Based program spends about $500 per student to provide services to Claribel and 400 other Dover High students actively enrolled in counseling, medical outreach, recreation, and vocational programs. Tiger RAP's annual $214,000 state-funded budget equals the amount it would have cost to keep Claribel's family in foster care until Manny and Manuela grow up. Although Claribel's victory is dramatic, her success is not atypical.

In 1991, New Jersey's School-Based program was honored by the Ford Foundation and Harvard's Kennedy School of Government as one of America's ten most innovative government programs. Along with programs like TAP in Washington State, the Center for Family Life in Brooklyn, Focus: HOPE in Detroit, and grass-roots efforts like the West Side Athletic and Cultural Club in Detroit and Father Boyle's parish in Los Angeles, School-Based exemplifies how Americans are helping teenagers cross over from childhood into adulthood. Coming of age in America need not be as difficult as it is.

THE FAMILY

GROUND ZERO OF AMERICAN POVERTY

The American family as we once knew it appears to be a threatened, if not endangered, species. Most children born today will grow up in broken families, and many single mothers and children will experience poverty. Being a parent too often means waking up with the fear that there isn't time to do all you need to do in the day, and going to bed with anxiety that you are failing as an employee, parent, and spouse. It means praying that you won't lose your job, because you'll also lose your health insurance; if you get sick, you could lose everything. It means depending on overwhelmed courts to settle marital disputes, and getting caught up in lawyers' confrontational tactics.

For children caught between warring parents in custody battles, it means being twisted in knots as their loyalties are divided. For the parent who moves out, it means isolation and loneliness, punctuated by guilt. For the parent who has custody, it means depending on a fragmented child-support system that doesn't work, waiting for checks that come erratically or not at all. For families headed by single women, it means losing money, power, and status, and as one author put it, "falling from grace."

It's hard to characterize the average American family, but even harder not to stereotype the poor. The popular conception that most poor families are black, inner-city welfare recipients is simply incorrect: "Ghetto poverty" constitutes less than 10 percent of total U.S. poverty, according to Professor David Ellwood of Harvard's Kennedy School of Government.

If you're an average poor family, you don't live on welfare—you work. You're white, you live in suburbia, and your children go to school with holes in their sneakers and return to an empty house entered with a latchkey. To support them, you work long hours for low wages and no benefits, and you still can't afford basics like food, clothes, housing, and transportation.

During the Reagan-Bush years, the average worker's paycheck shriveled in buying power to the size it was before the War on Poverty in the 1960s. In families where one parent worked, the poverty rate climbed by 30 percent between 1980 and 1990. Many military families need food stamps to afford groceries for their kids. If you work in a service industry—a fancy title for minimum-wage drudgery—you get no health insurance, so if you continue working, you are endangering your family's health. It's a temptation to go on welfare just to get Medicaid, but you fear the stigma.

The poorest of poor Americans are single parents with children. If you are a poor single mother, you are the lowest of the low in the new American caste system. Your children are treated like "bastards," as one senator puts it, and the government's provision for bastards is kept deliberately low to discourage you from having more babies.

As a welfare mother, you are stigmatized for dependency and blamed for many of America's most serious problems. You could turn on the television after the riots in Los Angeles and hear the vice-president (the same one who helped Cindy and Tim) blaming single mothers for fostering a "poverty of values" and "lawless social anarchy," when your neighborhood was the one that burned down, your children were the ones being shot, and California's governor was talking about cutting welfare by 25 percent—after welfare grants nationally had already diminished 40 percent since the 1970s.

Still, no single definition encompasses the American family: There is the never-divorced couple with two children, now a minority; the remarried couple with children in a new composite family; the single-parent family; the extended family; the skipped-generation family of grandparents raising grandchildren . . .

The stories in this chapter touch the lives of five families who plunged to the bottom, and the special few who found a way out. The stories explore white, middle-class mothers who slipped into poverty; a poor white widow; and African-American and Latina mothers who clawed their way out of extreme deprivation. One father died; another stood by his children; and most fathers abandoned their children.

These stories reveal facets of family life that have been ignored in debates on welfare fraud and family values. They are included here in the hope that they may correct misperceptions and reflect complex dangers facing families from every direction. The family, whether it supports its members or fails to function, is the hub of generations, the center of the life span.

Each family saga is unique: K.D.'s ex-husband preferred to send his sons postcards rather than child support; Billy Jean and Mary Lou were raising very different families in the same depressed neighborhood in East Tennessee; Tina's children endured sexual abuse and their mother's cocaine addiction in a housing project in Boston; Nitza, a third-generation welfare mother, lost her children and became homeless in New York City's South Bronx.

Their struggles show what families must endure to stay together, and how community programs help poor mothers help themselves. They counter the pernicious image of the welfare mother that has wreaked so much destruction, yet they do not gloss over human failings. They teach that there are no easy victories but, even in the most dire circumstances, there is what one mother calls "hard hope."

Sexual molestation is a thread that runs through three of the women's lives. Before hearing the testimony of women bearing witness in this book, I could not have predicted that sexual and physical abuse would be at the root of so many families' problems. I had assumed that poverty was linked to economic and social factors, not to psychological wounds. Yet, during scores of interviews conducted in different regions of the country, a surprising number of both middle-class and poor women revealed painful histories of incest and sexual abuse.

Sexual abuse is the dirty secret of American families at all income levels. As many as one-third of all girls and boys are abused before reaching adulthood. They are far more likely to fall into poverty, or remain trapped in it, than those who are not abused. Conversely, poor children who were never abused are more resilient and better able to fend for themselves as adults.

The best description of the impact of abuse is that "incest punches holes in the soul," explains Dr. Mary Dreyer, a California psychologist who has helped many survivors. The following stories have convinced me that the healing of the soul, whether through psychological treatment, prayer, or other means, is as much a part of fighting poverty as economic relief.

The prime cause of poverty in American families is the financial abandonment of children, mostly by absent fathers. According to a 1990 Census study, only half of the 5 million divorced women entitled to child support actually receive full payment. One-quarter of them get sporadic or partial payments; one-quarter get nothing. Nearly 3 million more women requested child support but never received a court-ordered award.

K.D. Barrett, a fifty-one-year-old clerk, thought she had the American dream until she awoke to a living nightmare of divorce. In the mid-1970s, K.D. lived in a $120,000 home in an upper-middle-class suburb of Los Angeles with her husband, a successful aerospace engineer, and two boys. The boys idolized their father, who was also their football coach and hero. Unbeknownst to them, he was having an affair at work. He grew a beard and started wearing an open shirt with a gold chain. Soon after the birth of his third son, he walked out on K.D., leaving her with a newborn in a new condo between escrows, while she recovered from a C-section and a hysterectomy.

She had no job, no financial resources, no place to go. K.D. got a job as an assistant manager of a Kentucky Fried Chicken outlet, returning from work to hear her children pleading, "Why did Daddy leave?" They faced the loneliness of the night praying their father would come back, but he never did. Instead, he moved in with a woman with three children of her own and adopted a new life-style, vacationing in Cancún and the Caribbean, and sending T-shirts inscribed "It's better in the Bahamas" to his emotionally and financially neglected children. K.D. was forced to move into a motel room crowded with three kids, a dog, and a bird.

According to K.D., her divorce settlement required her ex-husband to pay $350 a month in child support and $250 in spousal support. K.D.'s share of the $86,000 equity in their house was $13,000, which she spent in two years. She was supporting a family of four on $1,200 a month in 1979 and 1980. Four times her ex-husband escaped payment. Refusing to undergo the stigma of public assistance, K.D. managed never to go on welfare, relying instead on friends to loan her money to make it through each month. She was earning $5 an hour frying chicken while her ex-husband was earning $45 an hour designing aerospace technology.

After years of struggle, she is now supporting herself as a clerk at a municipal utility company in Sacramento, California, earning $2,000 a month. She lives in a rented condominium with her youngest son, who is doing well in high school. Her two oldest boys, who were hit hardest by the abandonment by their father, were "incorrigible" adolescents. One dropped out of school, got hooked on drugs, and lived for a disastrous period with his father. He straightened himself out by joining the navy, and later served in the Persian Gulf War. Her other son is now a customer service representative for a computer company, and still bears the scars of resentment.

In her fifties, K.D. feels young but has not yet become involved in another long-term relationship. She finds that most men her age are not enamored of a woman with three children. Rather than getting involved with the wrong person, she chooses to remain independent and self-sufficient. "I don't have diamond rings," she says proudly. "I have my dignity."

Divorce is the predictable crisis of American life, yet America has no social insurance for single parents and their children. A national system of child support—as advocated by Professor Ellwood of Harvard—that deducts payments directly from absent parents' wages could ensure children's security much as Social Security helps the elderly weather the ravages of old age.

For women and children, such a system has three distinct advantages: (1) It would collect revenue from the absent parent for a period of eighteen years; (2) it would have no stigma attached to it, since middle-class and poor families would receive their child-support payments through the system, much as Social Security recipients receive monthly checks; and (3) it would not be considered public assistance and thus would not prevent mothers from working—a significant advance over welfare.

In the absence of a family security system, millions of American families like K.D.'s experience extreme hardship that feels, tastes, and smells like poverty, but technically they never fall below the official U.S. poverty line. This is because the out-of-date poverty guidelines grossly underestimate the cost of keeping a family housed, clothed, fed, healthy, and provided with child care in the 1990s.

The so-called poverty line was created in the early 1960s by an obscure statistician working for the Social Security Administration. Using data from 1955, Mollie Orshansky estimated that most families spent about one-third of their income on food. She multiplied the government's basic food allotment by a factor of three to come up with the minimum amount of income necessary to support a family. Mollie says she had no intention of creating a poverty line.

But the Johnson administration adopted her standard in 1965, and it has been the official measure of poverty ever since. It is used to compute whether people are eligible for many government programs. The poverty line has been updated to compensate for monetary inflation, but the basic formula has not changed in a generation, even though the proportion of income American families spend on basics has radically changed. Today's families spend far more for housing and child care than in the past, now budgeting only one-fifth of their income for food. If the old poverty line were updated—by multiplying the food allotment by five instead of three—it would be a better standard for measuring the real poverty level today. But computing poverty based on food consumption is still rather arbitrary. What is a fair measure of poverty?

The Center on Budget and Policy Priorities, Washington's premier research institute on poverty issues, conducted a comprehensive national public opinion poll back in 1988, asking Americans from every region what was the minimum they could live on as a family. Using the public's own measures of poverty, which varied by region, the center found that about 45 million Americans were poor, compared to the 32 million Americans who were officially designated as poor. By 1991, the number of Americans living under the official poverty line—37.5 million people—reached its highest point since the beginning of the War on Poverty in 1964. But the real number was at least 24 percent higher—46.5 million Americans—according to the center's research director, Kathryn Porter.

Unlike many government statistics, the poverty line figures are susceptible to real-life comparisons. The official poverty line is $6,932 a year for an individual and $13,924 for a family of four. Living on these amounts is nearly impossible, yet entitlements for poor children and their parents do not even bring families up to poverty level. Either a new standard that reflects contemporary families' housing, child-care, medical, food, and transportation costs should be adopted, or the government should stop disseminating its Orwellian line on poverty.

A crucial threshold of poverty is not economic, but psychological. We know of rich families who are negligent in the way they treat their elders and children; we know of poor families who are close-knit and manage to achieve a lot with a little. These distinctions blur the economic borders of poverty but in no way erase them: The rich can buy their way out of many problems, but the poor must suffer both poverty and neglect.

The family may be described as an immune system protecting its members from violence, craziness, alienation, self-destructiveness—the ills of modern society. When the family is weak, people are more susceptible to virulent social behaviors that, in turn, further weaken the family in a spiral of self-destruction. The breakdown of the family is a sort of social immunodeficiency sydrome. Yet it need not be fatal.

To heal or create a family requires tremendous personal commitment, moral support, and *practical help from the community*. As pioneer families helped each other in barn raisings, family pioneers raise the roof beam of emotional support sheltering families from the wilderness of isolation.

A grass-roots organization located in the back of a church provides food baskets and other assistance to families in Oak Ridge, Tennessee. Aid to Distressed Families in Anderson County (ADFAC) serves a divided community composed of poor folk who have a high degree of illiteracy and scientists who developed the atomic bomb. Beginning with the Manhattan Project during World War II, the influx of federal nuclear-energy workers who came to Oak Ridge

139

fractured the social cohesion of the sleepy Appalachian community hidden in the smoke-blue hills. This process of social mobility and family breakdown was duplicated across the United States following the Second World War.

The Director of ADFAC, Carol Siemens, came to Oak Ridge with her scientist husband in the 1980s. Trained as a social worker in Washington, D.C., Siemens discovered that most of the Tennessee families she tried to help were assailed by alcoholism, illiteracy, and constant fighting with their neighbors. Their poverty was endemic, ingrained in the culture like the plaintive voices of church choirs wailing in the pine woods in the rain; infant mortality was as old as the cherub tombstones standing on the hillsides behind white frame churches.

Although ADFAC's founder won a commendation from the Bush White House as an official Point of Light, the limits of volunteer work were hauntingly obvious to Carol as she made her rounds in Appalachia's hollows. The woods were dark with coal soot and tumbledown shacks; there weren't any doctors to deliver babies, let alone provide prenatal care; children suffered malnutrition; wives were abused, and their husbands enraged and powerless; poor families were broken apart by welfare policies that demanded that fathers abandon their wives and children.

This was the poverty Michael Harrington described so passionately in *The Other America* and, before him, James Agee and Walker Evans depicted in *Let Us Now Praise Famous Men*. It was—and is—a poverty that haunts America thirty years after Harrington called on the country to launch what would become the War on Poverty, and sixty years after Agee and Evans would call for the compassion of the New Deal. Poverty was partially reduced by those efforts, although the public doubted their effectiveness. Soon politicians found excuses to forget the neediest Americans, and Lyndon Johnson chose to escalate the war in Vietnam rather than win the War on Poverty.

Watching the campfires of homeless families flickering like fallen stars in the poor hollows of Appalachia, Carol Siemens believed that President Bush's public-relations campaign to award Points of Light to volunteer programs was no substitute for an effective, national program to alleviate poverty. Rather than taking refuge in apathy or despair, she chose to be involved in the struggle to help families find homes, food, and shelter; and though she often felt frustrated, she found that helping families was deeply rewarding. Among the mothers she assisted were two women living in the same public housing project.

Billie Jean was the daughter of a nuclear engineer, and raised in a middle-class Catholic family. A victim of incest, reportedly by an older brother, she rebelled against her parents, got pregnant in high school, left home, and fell on hard times. Striking bottom, Billie Jean found hope in a Christian prayer group. Through church activities, she visited a state prison where she met a convict named Harley, the only man to come to her prayer meeting. Impressed by her faith, Harley underwent a religious awakening. They married and started their family when he was still in prison. Out on parole after eight years, Harley was now struggling to make a new life with his wife and children.

Mary Lou was the daughter of an out-of-work coal miner. Born into poverty, she grew up in the hollows in a wooden shack with no running water. Her earliest memories were of trying to scrounge for food and being beaten by her stepfather, who kept the best morsels for himself. She married an older man, a Korean War veteran. He died when their five children were young, and she received survivor's benefits. Illiterate, she had a hard time managing their affairs. Her children looked hungry.

The two women lived in cramped housing units in wooden barracks left over from the Manhattan Project. But Billie Jean's house and children were immaculate; Mary Lou's house—which I visited without proper notice, before she had a chance to straighten things up—was littered with dirty clothing and smelled of cats, while her children looked bedraggled.

Carol Siemens faced different challenges in helping these two women and their families. Billie Jean was struggling to build up her marriage with Harley; he was having a hard time adjusting from prison, where he had served eight years for armed robbery. She needed someone to believe in her and give her advice and counseling. Intelligent and well-spoken, Billie Jean was highly motivated and capable. Harley also seemed determined to make a clean break from his past—he was a neglected child of a broken family—and be a good father, husband, and provider. But soon after Harley got out of prison, his father came to stay in the cramped house, thereby adding to Billie Jean's problems.

Three houses away, Mary Lou needed basics: food, clothing, and medicine. She would turn up at ADFAC periodically and get provisions for her family. But when Carol visited the widow's house, she found the children looking gaunt and acting out of control. Mary Lou's oldest son was emotionally disturbed and went around the house in his underwear, bellowing. To Carol's eyes, Mary Lou was clearly overwhelmed by the responsibility of raising her children. But, clearly, they loved their mother. Carol thought it was better to help Mary Lou cope than to split up the family and put the children in foster care.

When Carol took me to visit these two families in 1990, Mary Lou and her children looked hopeless, mired in poverty that perpetuated itself from generation to generation. In contrast, Harley had a good job. He and Billie

Jean were paying off their debts, hoping to move out of public housing and buy their first home.

In Billie Jean's case, hope and commitment for her family worked like a nuclear chain reaction in reverse. Carol helped Billie Jean get counseling for her sexual abuse, which lay at the root of her self-destructive behavior. The trust between Carol and Billie Jean reinforced the commitment between Billie Jean and Harley to make their marriage work.

"There is a way out of a hole," Billie Jean told me. "What's the secret? Perseverance. You got four kids. Divorce is not an option, cut it out of your vocabulary." She paused and gazed tenderly at her children, conceived behind bars when their father was in prison. "God never closes a door unless he opens a window."

In 1990, it seemed—on the surface at least—that Billie Jean and Harley's family had a better chance of making it out of poverty than Mary Lou and her fatherless children. Gaunt and wrinkled, holding her hollow-eyed son in her arms for me to take a snapshot, Mary Lou looked like a portrait of Appalachia unchanged from the Great Depression: eternally proud but poor.

The problems faced by impoverished white families in Appalachia are not the same as those suffered by destitute black families trapped in housing projects in the Northeast. No ethnic group has suffered more damage to its family structure than African-Americans, whose ancestors were torn from tribal communities, enslaved, raped, humiliated, abused, sold down the river; and whose forefathers and -mothers came north in the great migration to black ghettos in the industrial cities.

The effects last to this day. Indeed, the most destructive legacies of both slavery and migration were to break the human chain of child-rearing traditions binding African-Americans into close-knit kinship groups.

There is a debate among social scientists whether the breakdown of the black family is the result of slavery, oppression, discrimination, and lack of jobs, or whether it is caused by entitlement programs that promote welfare dependency. Both sides have evidence to back them up. Still, the debate itself has become unproductive, because it is used to blame and avoid responsibility rather than to recognize the reality that all of these factors harm black families.

A note of caution: Anyone who believes that these problems are confined to blacks in the inner cities is mistaken. The same process of family breakdown that Senator Daniel Patrick Moynihan described for the black family in the early 1960s is now striking the white family in the 1990s.

Ironically, at a time when *all* families are more vulnerable, cutbacks in education, health, and social services have decimated the support systems families need. Basic institutions that once supported the middle class and helped raise families out of poverty are now falling below the institutional poverty line—unable to function efficiently to provide vital services. Whites who need public services are now suffering the bitter experience of blacks who learned not to depend on the government. If social services can't be trusted, and families can't make it alone, where can people turn?

In the Lincoln Towers housing project near Boston, white, Latino, and black families living in a bitter wasteland of drugs, gang violence, and welfare poverty turn to the Family Center. This cozy community center, similar to Sunset Park's Center for Family Life but on a smaller scale, focuses on the strengths of families rather than their weaknesses.

The center is run by Anne Peretz, a committed family therapist with a degree in social work. After working on grass-roots programs for years, Anne came to see families as the forefront of the struggle against violence, drugs, and poverty. The main counseling center is located in a Victorian house in Somerville, Massachusetts. A small satellite office in the bleak, brick Lincoln housing project helps families deal with the problems assailing them from every direction. It is staffed by Family Center social worker Sandra Brown, a black woman who grew up in Manchester, England, and who still has a soft English accent.

For the past seven years, Sandra has been working with an African-American mother named Tina, her four children, and one of their absent fathers to build a family structure out of the chaos—a family that fulfills their needs, not an arbitrary mold. Tina was orphaned as a child and raised by a strict aunt; her uncle molested her sexually for several years. Escaping from the prison of incest, she dropped out of school, had children with different fathers, and became addicted to crack cocaine.

To an outside observer, Tina reflected the problems of a welfare mother trapped in a near-suicidal response to abuse and poverty. But Sandra Brown searched for the family's strengths—and found them in Tina's love for her children, and their refusal to let their mother destroy herself with drugs.

Tina contacted the Family Center after an incident in which she became so enraged at her little boy, Rob, for spreading peanut butter and jelly all over the kitchen, she nearly strangled him. Tina realized she needed help and went voluntarily to the Family Center. Soon, she and the children were involved in child-abuse prevention, support groups, and recreational activities. The family interventions over the next several years involved all aspects of their lives, but three events show how counseling deals with psychosocial problems that are beyond the scope of economic assistance or judicial punishment.

The first came in January 1987, after Sandra observed suspicious drug activity in Tina's apartment. Tina was very thin and often wore two or three layers of clothing to hide her emaciated body. Her eyes were glassy—a telltale sign of cocaine use. Sandra decided to try a drug intervention with Tina but, instead of facing the addicted woman alone, where she could deny using drugs, Sandra chose to confront Tina within earshot of her children.

"I think you're doing drugs and you don't trust me enough to let me know—to come clean," Sandra began. "It seems drugs are more important to you than working with your children and me at the Family Center," she said loudly. Tina's children, who were in the next room, could hear their mother being confronted. Sandra threatened to pull the children out of recreation programs unless Tina got into drug therapy. This was a risky move, for the children loved participating, but Sandra counted on the children's desire to stay involved with the Family Center—their only source of emotional support—to pressure Tina to get treatment.

A week later, a drug customer knocked on the door of Tina's apartment. Emboldened by having overheard his mother being challenged about her drug abuse, Tina's son Rob, who was just ten, refused to open the door.

"I don't know what's going on, Mommy," Rob pleaded. "But if it doesn't stop, or you don't stop it, I will!" the distraught boy shouted at his mother. He threatened to call the child protection agency for help if she didn't put herself in treatment. Tina faced the awful choice of losing her children or giving up her addiction. She made the choice to preserve her family, and the Family Center orchestrated practical measures that helped her stop using and selling drugs. Tina entered a drug detox center for only two days, then started attending outpatient therapy meetings. The threat of losing her children spurred her on. At one point, when Tina wavered, Sandra even confronted the neighborhood pusher and convinced him to stop selling drugs to Tina. These efforts succeeded: Since February 1987, Tina has remained clean of drugs. But the reasons she relied on drugs in the first place lay much deeper, preventing her from functioning as a mother.

The second event occurred in the spring of 1987, after Tina had stopped using drugs. She had joined a support group for women. In a private counseling session, Anne Peretz helped Tina and her daughter Monique confront the terrible secret of sexual abuse. Monique confided she had been fondled by a teenage girl at camp. Tina's first reaction was to lash out angrily at her daughter, as if it were her fault, instead of trying to comfort her. Anne sensed that Tina was reexperiencing something horrible from her own childhood that prevented her from feeling compassion for her daughter.

To help them communicate, Anne asked Tina, who was taller than her daughter, to sit in a small chair. She asked Monique to sit in a big chair. With their eyes nearly level, she asked them to draw forward and face each other, so close that two fists barely separated their knees. With her eyelashes shining with tears, Monique looked away, afraid of her mother's piercing gaze. Gently, Anne asked Monique to let her mother know what she was feeling in her heart.

"I can't feel your pain, Mommy, because I'm hurting," Monique wept. Tina also started to cry. Her gaunt cheeks, ravaged by years of drug abuse, became puffy, and her taut lower lip, which usually held back emotions, crumpled, and she began to sob.

147

Anne asked Tina to look deeply into her daughter's eyes and imagine she was gazing into a mirror. "I see me at eight, when a man came into the room at night . . ." Tina moaned, as the memories of repeated incestual rapes flooded back from childhood in her aunt's house. Her entire body trembled, releasing the memories she had kept in all these years. Gently, Anne suggested that she may be punishing her daughter because she was angry at herself for having been abused as a child, but that it wasn't either of their faults. Tina nodded, the catharsis bringing her closer to her daughter, whose smooth face reflected her own ravaged visage.

Later in the session, Anne had the two of them switch big and small chairs to realize that, though they resembled each other, one was the mother and the other the daughter. The therapy session was a crucial step in what became a long, painful process of healing that continues to this day.

Its immediate impact was to help prevent further molestations. A few weeks later, Tina's drunk boyfriend, Big Chris, entered a darkened bedroom, slipped his hand under Monique's nightgown, and started fondling her. Terrified, she got out of bed and went to another room, but she didn't tell her mother what had happened, fearing the consequences. After keeping it secret for two weeks, however, Monique finally confided everything to Sandra Brown, the social worker who had become her friend. In clipped English, Sandra stood up to the accused child molester, telling Big Chris in no uncertain terms to meet her at Tina's apartment for a talk. She then told Tina. Anguished, Tina cried, "I know he did it! That's what he does to me, too; when he thinks I'm asleep, he'll crawl under the covers and have sex."

The next day, shielded by women who supported her, Monique sat on the couch between the social worker and her mother, who held her hand. Plopping uncomfortably on a hard chair, the accused molester sat facing them, as if in court.

"Big Chris, Monique is here to tell you something," Sandra began. In a trembling voice, Monique described awakening two weeks before to find him pulling down the covers and touching her vagina. Shifting nervously in his seat, Chris brushed it off, saying he'd been drinking and stumbled in the dark; perhaps his hand had touched her by accident. But Tina, reaching inside for strength, spoke up: "I know you did it, Chris, from the way Monique described it."

Chris protested he had done nothing wrong, but the women would not back down. Finally, he apologized: "If I did something to disrespect you, I'm sorry." Before leaving the meeting, he agreed never to be alone in the apartment with Monique. As a result of this face-to-face confrontation, Tina and Monique felt better able to protect their bodies—and those of the three other children. Learning how to defend herself, what Sandra called "developing internal boundaries," helped Tina gain courage to venture out of the housing project into the Boston area. As she felt safer, the spark returned to her eyes, the flesh returned to her bones, and her confidence began to bloom. Turning her skill at selling drugs to better use, she landed a sales job at a prestigious store near Harvard Square and began supporting her children with a paycheck for the first time.

Still, she was a single parent fulfilling the emotional needs of her four children, while their three absent fathers ignored them. It was not enough to come clean of drugs and heal the wounds of the past; she needed to build a family structure for her children, and somehow enlist the fathers to assume their male roles—especially for the boys who needed them so deeply.

The third event took place nearly a year later, after Tina was clean of drugs and working. She brought her former lover, José, to the Family Center for a meeting with his natural son, Joselito. The boy, who was seven, sat between his mother and Matt Cibula, the leader of the center's group for boys, and a graduate of Harvard. José sat uneasily on a chair with everyone looking at him.

Joselito spoke up, recounting the times that his father had failed to come to his birthday party and to his school. "You just don't care and I hate you!" Joselito said. Then Tina spoke up, telling José that his son was hurting himself and threatening to jump out the window. "What are you going to do?" she demanded.

There was nowhere for José to hide. He faced his son and promised to spend more time with him. "When?" demanded Joselito. Together, they drew up a contract pledging that José would regularly visit his son and take him places as a father. José signed it. For six months he followed through, but then José went back to Puerto Rico, abandoning Joselito once more.

Of all the problems facing families like Tina's, the problem of abandonment by fathers is the most crippling financially and the most difficult for society to remedy. The Family Center could only draft a voluntary contract binding father to son—an artificial substitute for the male bonding that was absent, a worthless piece of paper when it came down to enforcing the financial responsibility José had for the little boy he had fathered.

Without a father, a boy is far more likely to reject authority at school and join a gang, hoping to find a role model to make up for his missing father. The tendency is also greater to abuse himself and to attack others—and to father children whom he, in turn, abandons. The cycle of fathers abandoning sons who later abuse women and abandon children is the male component of the "welfare mother" cycle, but it has conveniently been swept under the rug, while welfare mothers are left holding the bag for our entire society's abandonment of families.

The Family Center alone cannot make up for the failings of José and Big Chris, or the weaknesses of Tina, but it is doing a lot. Rob, who played such an important role in his mother's quitting drugs, is making it out of the housing project into the larger world. He now attends a private and prestigious college-preparatory school on scholarship. Not all of Tina's children may make it, but the efforts of Sandra Brown and Anne Peretz in behalf of this family show the commitment of grass-roots organizations. They also show the transformative power of therapy to help a family confront the internal crises wrenching it apart.

The most vulnerable of all families are homeless mothers and children forced into the streets, separated by their would-be protectors, and blown like dust by the whirlwind. The stereotype of America's homeless population, whose number even eludes the U.S. Census, is a single person who was kicked out of a mental hospital, raving on a street corner. In reality, many state mental hospitals closed long ago. Though perhaps one-third of the homeless are mentally unstable—the result, sometimes, of the bitter experience of homelessness—many are neither insane nor single. They are families with young children.

This is the story of a third-generation Latina welfare mother who was battered and forced onto the streets, who lost her children and wandered homeless for three years. It is a story of survival in the face of abandonment that is consuming the American family and turning once-thriving communities into urban wildernesses.

Nitza was born at ground zero of American poverty, the

South Bronx. The neighborhood is less than half an hour by subway from Manhattan's posh Upper East Side, but before the northbound train reaches Harlem, virtually all whites exit. Beyond Yankee Stadium lies a no-man's-land of gutted buildings and derelict parks ravening with rats.

Nitza's childhood was filled with beatings, molestations, and grinding poverty. Born in 1958 to a Puerto Rican mother and a Spanish father, she was the eldest of five children and a second-generation heir to welfare. Seven people lived in one furnished room of a second-floor tenement, and it seemed a baby was always crying. By the time Nitza was eight, she was responsible for taking care of her five younger sisters and brothers. When she failed, she was beaten by her father. He wore a thick, brown leather belt that he whipped out with one hand while grabbing Nitza with the other. She still remembers the sound as it slipped through the loops. He beat her buttocks, her legs, her back, her arms, beating and beating until she cried hard enough to satisfy him. Once, she couldn't catch her breath, and her mother shouted to shut up or she would beat her, too.

Nitza found refuge in school, where her first-grade teacher encouraged her to draw and paint. When her crayon slipped outside the lines, she expected to get a beating, as she would at home; instead, the teacher patiently showed her how to draw within the lines. Nitza excelled in school, but at home was not encouraged to study. After all, she was only a girl and she was expected to follow in her mother's footsteps, to get married, raise children, and submit to her husband.

Nitza's body was violated when she was four years old. She remembers playing with her friend Maya, who lived on the ground floor of the same tenement. One evening, Nitza wanted to play with Maya's cherished tea set, but Maya's father suggested they play hide-and-seek. He seemed warm and nice to Nitza, not cold and distant like her own father. Maya hid first, then it was Nitza's turn. "Why don't you hide in the closet?" he suggested. Nitza tried to find the darkest corner so Maya wouldn't find her, but the man was already in the closet. He grabbed Nitza's waist and began exploring her body. At first she thought it was a different kind of game, then she grew tense and numb. Afterward, she felt guilty and ugly.

Nitza stopped going to Maya's apartment, but the molester started coming over to visit Nitza's father. Once, when Nitza was lying on the couch watching TV, Maya's dad sat down on the hassock near her. Before she could get up, he asked Nitza's father for a screwdriver. As Nitza's father went to look in the kitchen, the man began stroking her. Nitza was terrified that her father would see what was happening—and beat her. If she complained, she feared he'd get mad and beat her anyway. So she kept silent.

She kept her silence for years, while being molested by a series of friends' fathers, neighbors, and older boys. At twelve, she finally broke down and told a trusted family friend about the molestations. But no one believed her. Nitza never spoke up again to her family, though she was molested dozens of times.

At seventeen, she dropped out of school and got pregnant by the first man who showed her affection. She became his common-law wife, only to discover he treated her like her father and was shiftless, refusing to work or support his children. Passive and powerless, with a diminished self-image and few expectations, she seemed to fit the mold of the third-generation welfare mother.

But Nitza refused to be a statistic. Eight months pregnant with her fourth child, she watched her young children go hungry while their father played numbers with food stamps and drank the welfare check. When she protested, he beat her, just as her drunken father had beaten her as a child, then used her body numbed by abuse.

Nitza struggled to free herself. She went to the welfare office and begged them to take his name off the public assistance checks so the money could go to her children. In New York, fathers are permitted to live with families receiving welfare, and the clerk said he would have to come down to the office and remove his name himself. "Why would he do that?" the distraught mother protested. But rules are rules, and so her live-in husband collected Aid to Families with Dependent Children (AFDC) while she and the children starved.

A year after the birth of their fourth child, she was battered and abandoned by this man. Even with welfare, monthly payments had been cut so deeply that Nitza's family was living about 20 percent below the official poverty level in New York City. When the welfare checks stopped coming to her, there was no cushion of savings. In Nitza's case, the effect was devastating—no money for food or rent.

First they turned off the lights, then they evicted Nitza and her children. She didn't want them thrown on the street. A priest advised her to put them in "voluntary placement"—foster care—until she could find another apartment and get her welfare established independently. She gathered her four children—ages seven, five, three, and one—around her.

She told them she was sick and was going to a hospital, and that she was sending them to live at a friend's house for a little while. She had never lied to them before, and they believed her. She dressed them and took them to the 46th Precinct police station, not because she had broken a law, but because the police were to turn the children over to the foster-care agency.

"Don't worry, as soon as I'm better, we'll be together again," she told them. Watching the police put them in the rear seat of the cruiser, Nitza cried, "Carmen, hold Yvette! Make sure she doesn't fall." Then the cruiser pulled out and Nitza watched her children drive away, looking back at their mother growing smaller and smaller through the rear window.

That night she slept in a park. She went for four days on nothing but coffee. Drug dealers would tempt her, urging, "I can fix your problem." Maybe if she sold crack she could earn money and get her kids fast. She was also tempted by prostitution. But each time, a voice inside her warned that going down those roads might forever separate her from her children; Nitza chose hunger and homelessness.

Nitza lived for one thing: reuniting her family. She was determined to find a new home and get her children back as quickly as possible. But she confronted a Kafkaesque array of inflexible regulations that were supposedly designed to prevent welfare fraud. The welfare office told her that because her children were in foster care, she no longer qualified for AFDC. Landlords said she couldn't get an apartment because she had no welfare income. She couldn't go to a job interview because in the course of her homelessness, she had lost her clothes.

Unlike the lax enforcement enjoyed by her husband, Nitza was hounded off welfare. She became caught in the cycle of homelessness, along with countless other poor families victimized by the system that was supposed to protect them.

Nitza's children joined 40,000 others in New York's overburdened foster-care system, a city within a city of displaced boys and girls shuffled from home to home, many never to return to their parents. Nitza was so desperate to see and reassure her children that, in a moment of weakness, she took the money given to buy clothing for herself and spent it on toys for the kids. She went to the foster agency and waited in vain for the children to come, until the office closed and she was shooed onto the street.

The times when she did see them, parting was painful. She would get up and they would begin grabbing her legs and crying, "Don't leave, Mommy!" They developed a parting ritual of waving, blowing kisses, and saying "I love you" for as long as they were in sight.

Nitza's children were well cared for by foster parents, but their mother never knew if they would be moved to another home, or if she would lose them forever. When she was destitute, the foster-care agency gave Nitza subway tokens to visit her children every two weeks. She cashed in the tokens, walked three hours to the visitation center, and used the money to buy candy for her kids. Nitza's sole source of pride during the bleakest period of her life was that she went two and a half years without missing one appointment with her children.

Nitza's psychological state was devastated by her wanderings on the streets, but she was no crazier than the system that destroys families in order to save them. Apparently, no one in any of the government agencies that touched her file looked at the needs of Nitza and her children as a whole family; no one asked her what basic tools she needed in order to shelter and support her young ones; no one believed that she was capable of supporting herself, much less four children . . . until she walked into the Citizens Advice Bureau and met Myrna Perez.

The Citizens Advice Bureau, a community antipoverty agency, is unique in New York City and, perhaps, America. It was modeled on Citizens Advice Bureaus in England: neighborhood service centers where people go for advice and aid. The Citizens Advice Bureau in the Bronx is now twenty years old. Carolyn McLaughlin, executive director, was there from the beginning.

"People come here with problems—housing, welfare, entitlements, domestic violence—or looking for jobs," says the willowy director with a social work degree from Columbia. "We deal with the problems of day-to-day living for poor people."

Every year, about 20,000 people receive services directly from the bureau's nine storefront offices. The nonprofit agency raises its $1.3 million annual budget from an array of community, civic, and private sources. The policy is: No appointments. No requirements. Anyone can come in with any question and the bureau tries to sort out their problems, as Myrna did when Nitza asked for help.

Myrna Perez had come up the hard way herself, growing up in a poor but intact Puerto Rican family, and though she had no extensive training in social work, she had an intuitive ability to listen to people and respond. Myrna helped poor clients who came into the bureau for advice in a way that did not rob them of their dignity; nor did she try to fit them into categories and give them superficial solutions.

Facing her awkwardly on a wooden chair, Myrna found a disheveled, bedraggled Puerto Rican woman in her twenties who smelled bad from living on the streets. Her skin was sallow and her flesh hung on her. Nitza seemed ashamed of her appearance as a bag lady, and her large, soft eyes looked hungry for forgiveness and approval. Myrna listened to Nitza's story, hearing a distraught Roman Catholic mother confessing her sins—she had brought children into the world and failed to protect them, had lost her children, and was unable to support herself. She listened, and when Nitza stopped pouring

out the reasons why she deserved the fate of being homeless, Myrna said, "I don't think you're all bad. I see good
in you."

It was the first time Nitza could remember that someone believed in her, not because she looked like she was
coping—she was depressed and dirty—but because
Myrna believed that in a mother's capacity for love there
was the strength necessary to fight the system, regain her
self-respect, and win back her children. This was commu-
nicated in a moment's gesture, amid a room filled with
scores of people waiting for help, each with a different
travail and a different need. There was no evidence of the
impact of Myrna's words on the seemingly helpless wreck
of a woman sitting on the folding chair beside the beat-
up desk. Certainly, no social scientist could measure the
effect of this interaction, and few politicians would justify
funding a program that provided nothing more concrete
than advice.

But Nitza would later credit Myrna's faith in her, a
total stranger, for giving her the first justification to have
faith in herself. The words were spoken as Myrna wrote
down the address or phone number of some agency where
Nitza could apply for help—neither woman remembers
what the practical advice was—but the effect was like
that of a mountain rescuer driving a piton in a cliff where
a lost climber clung above the abyss. The deep connection gave Nitza a point of security from which to climb.

Nitza disappeared into the streets, finding refuge in a
homeless shelter. Periodically she returned for another
bit of advice, another moment of reassurance.

The first step was a job. The Citizens Advice Bureau
had a job-referral system, and it helped people like Nitza
who had never applied for a position. As it turned out,
the job Nitza found was in a lawyer's office that was
doing a land-office business evicting families like her own

from rat-infested apartments. Once the buildings were emptied, they could be torched to collect fire insurance. She lied to the lawyer that she had legal experience and could type a zillion words per minute—and landed the job. She taught herself to type legal forms at night and spent the moments when the boss was out of the office calling the people who were to be evicted and warning them. It was a small consolation.

Working at the law office for one year, she attended night classes at Fordham University, even though she had only completed ninth grade and didn't have a high school diploma. She saved every dollar until she had enough to rent a small apartment. Then she went back to Myrna, who was now becoming not only an adviser but a friend, and she found out about a gutted apartment building that was being rehabbed. Myrna helped her apply, and Nitza was put on a waiting list that eventually produced an apartment she could afford.

This is how the Citizens Advice Bureau works. It has no benefits to hand out, no entitlements to give, no stern lectures to preach. It provides advice on the most practical details of daily living; it also provides a human connection for people stymied by the system. The service rendered Nitza is part of a $50,000-a-year contract funded by the City of New York that employs three counselors providing assistance to 800 people a year. That's $62 per person—a pittance for a chance to turn someone's life around. The equipment is simple to say the least: five or six wooden desks, with a chair for the social worker and one each for the clients, and a waiting room where maybe two dozen chairs were occupied. The office is cold, and often in winter the power goes out and they are plunged into darkness. To Nitza, however, the candles they used were a fireplace of human warmth from the cold of the streets.

The office is in an old apartment house on the Grand Concourse, where middle-class families once promenaded and now poverty gapes from gutted tenements. In the back is a wood-paneled ballroom with chairs stacked upside-down on tables, and a cracked window. If you squint through the window, you can imagine what the Grand Concourse looked like in the early part of the century, when people like Mollie Orshansky, who later invented the poverty line, went to school in the immigrant neighborhood.

Nitza told her social worker she now had a job, savings, and an apartment. A discharge date was made for her children to return home. First came her daughter Carmen, who was neurologically impaired and had been institutionalized at the Bronx Children's Psychiatric Center. Nitza took her to dinner at McDonald's to celebrate. The next week, her three other children arrived, excited to have a home and a united family at last. Nitza pasted a "Welcome Home" sign on the wall and placed gifts for them around the room. After three hard years, she had brought her family together.

Nitza and her children moved into the rehabbed apartment building across the street from Carolyn McLaughlin's office. Nitza got a job at the bureau as an information specialist, earning $17,000 a year. Her mentor, Myrna Perez, became her boss. As part of her work, Nitza goes to the woman's shelter where she once lived and recruits other women to enroll in job training programs. People who saw her knocking on doors as a homeless mother now see her working at the Citizens Advice Bureau—a powerful role model. When a client comes in for a housing application or a utility bill, she doesn't just give them information. She maps routes out of the labyrinth of poverty.

In 1991, ten years after Nitza first entered the Citizens

Advice Bureau, I visited her family in the South Bronx. Three of her four kids are at home one evening after work and school. In the living room, there are the mementos of Nitza's success: matching couches covered with plastic, and photos of her three daughters and son. In front of the television, which is hooked up to a Nintendo, is a row of library books. The books reflect the children's dreams: Carmen, fifteen, wants to be a veterinarian. Rosa, fourteen, wants to be an attorney for animal rights. Raymond, twelve, wants to be an archaeologist or discover the cure for AIDS. Yvette, ten, wants to be a social worker and help foster children.

"I broke six cycles," says Nitza, counting her personal victories on the fingers of two hands. She names them in a rhythmic litany: "The cycle of sexual child abuse; the cycle of physical child abuse; the cycle of domestic violence; the cycle of welfare, third generation; the cycle of homelessness; the cycle of victimization." Her hands close into a fist of determination.

"And I'm still fighting."

MID-LIFE

LEE, JOE ALLEN, AND JEAN

The brutal changes in our economy as America padlocks basic industries and slumps into the postindustrial era bear down heavily on people in middle age. Millions of Americans who worked hard, saved their money, and raised their children find themselves suddenly unemployed and uninsured. They lose not only their jobs and health insurance, but their dignity and even their lives.

The 75 million Americans who are now reaching mid-life grew up in a self-sufficient nation that poured its own steel, built its own cars, and consumed its own products. But as America entered the global marketplace, economic independence disappeared. Veteran U.S. workers are now forced to compete against foreign workers half their age who work for a fraction of their wages. As children, these Americans got better health care than any prior generation, but self-employed adults can't afford to pay for health insurance.

People in mid-life feel insecure, not because they are crazy, but sane: Their jobs are less secure than their parents'. Their achievements, no matter how significant, fall short of the inflated expectations they were given as children in the 1950s. Their horizons are diminishing while their burdens are growing. Americans in their forties and fifties face different aspects of this generational crisis, and when problems hit, each person feels isolated and alone.

Middle-aged Americans also feel overtaxed and don't want to support wasteful federal social programs. But tax cuts didn't make the government more efficient. Instead, spending freezes starved the network of public institutions—like schools, libraries, and clinics—that middle-aged Americans rely on, making the daily business of life harder, not easier.

America is now spending its resources to pay the interest on its $4 trillion debt, and this creates a hidden "tax" on our entire economic system. When basic institutions fall beneath the poverty line, communities go bankrupt and human capital is wasted. People in the prime of life watch their children being neglected and their parents being squeezed, and they fear for their own future.

But unlike the very young and the very old, people in middle age are not powerless. They stand at the fulcrum of our society. They have the power to tip the crushing weight off the shoulders of the weakest and most vulnerable Americans, and move it back into balance. Wary of extremes, tired of promises, they are looking for a middle way. They are America's past and future merging in the defining moment of their lives.

The following stories explore fundamental insecurities of mid-life: losing a job, getting sick, taking care of an aging parent. In each case, practical ways exist to help people survive such predictable crises, if only our society made them available.

Two men working hard in America's heartland were unaware of the shifts going on beneath the placid surface of their lives, one in a factory town, the other in the countryside. Lee Sliwinski, a fifty-one-year-old factory worker in Michigan, believed that his job with Firestone Steel made him secure for life. Joe Allen Bennett, a forty-nine-year-old farmer in Tennessee, took care of his sick parents and thought he deserved the same treatment. In the grip of forces beyond their control, these two strong-shouldered men both felt powerless as straws in the wind.

The mid-life crisis of Lee Sliwinski is an archetypal story of America's passage from innocence to hard experience in the postindustrial age. Like all adult crises, Lee's story begins with the expectations of childhood.

Now balding but still powerful as a bear, Lee remembers his childhood in the golden age of the American automobile industry. Lee was born in 1941, the year Japan attacked Pearl Harbor, and he grew up in Wyandotte, Michigan, a blue-collar suburb of Detroit that would later be devastated by the Japanese auto invasion.

Lee's family lived right across from a scrapyard. There could be no more fascinating a place for a boy than to glimpse machines chomping scrap metal like dinosaurs munching prehistoric plants. Twenty-three factories lined the Detroit River, their coal furnaces pumping soot from towering smokestacks into the sulfur-yellow sky. Wyandotte was the muscle and blood of Detroit's steel industry.

His dad, the son of Polish immigrants, worked as a boiler repairman at the Pennsylvania Salt Company, one of the big factories by the river. The family's life revolved around the factory, church, and the company bowling alley, where Lee set pins for twelve cents a line. The Sliwinskis were Lutherans who worked hard, without complaint or questions. From his earliest days, Lee's goals were to get a job and raise a family. That's all he wanted in life.

Lee came of age in the 1950s and he "liked Ike," because President Eisenhower was strong and fatherly, even though he was considered a "union-busting" Republican. In those days, everything seemed to be going right for America.

Blue-collar workers were the backbone of America's industrial might, and Lee absorbed their values in his bones. He respected authority and did what was required—no more, no less. He didn't make waves, didn't rock the boat, didn't overexcel, didn't ask questions. Lee heard about rugged individualism in civics class, but it was just an abstraction. What was real was to be part of a team—not to put himself ahead of others, but to cooperate. From birth, he was prepared to work on an assembly line. Letting other people do the thinking, the factory worker learned to repeat a mechanical job. It was like setting pins, a routine that became part of his makeup. He could do it in his sleep. He reserved his energy for having fun, playing ball, and horsing around with the kids, or mowing the lawn and fixing up the house.

The neighborhood was an extension of his living room, and its people were his people. They looked and talked and acted like him, and shared his values, his hopes, his fears, and his obligations. If he got in a fight, there were friends to set him right, and if he got in trouble drinking, his family was there to get him back on track. There were jobs for everybody who was willing to work. If a man was out of work in those days, it meant he was a lazy good-for-nothing. But if he worked too fast or hard, he might show up his pals, and that was no good either—a violation of the code of fellowship learned from childhood. A union worker didn't cheat the system. He supported it and it supported him. If he treated everybody equal, did an honest day's work, and raised a family, he'd be all right.

Maybe the air stank of pollutants, maybe the water was so dirty Lee could walk on it, maybe the houses in Wyandotte weren't as big as the mansions of the auto execs in Grosse Point. People born, bred, and raised downriver knew who they were. And they knew what made America from the bolts on up. Heavy industry built the country and they built the vehicles that ran it. By necessity, production caused waste, but labor unions made sure that industry scrapped metal, not people. American products were best. In the fifties, anything labeled "Made in Japan" was junk. Who could have imagined that those dinky Japanese cars that putt-putted around like motorcycles would doom Lee's future?

When Lee graduated from high school in 1959, his father bought him a black '55 Ford. More important, he used his influence to put his son's name on a hiring list at the steel plant where he was then working. He wanted his broad-shouldered boy to follow in his footsteps, and everyone expected Lee to follow through. Over six feet tall, with the grace of a varsity baseball player, Lee was the pride of his family and the bearer of their dreams. On the day after he graduated from high school, with his mind set on a secure future in a growing industry, Lee Sliwinski combed his hair back in a ducktail, drove his Ford down to the steel yard, and signed up. He got a $75-a-week job and thought he was set for life.

Thirty-two years later, Lee Sliwinski stands in front of the padlocked Firestone Steel plant in Wyandotte. Still powerfully built, but with his domed head now bald and his shoulders hunched over, favoring a back injured by heavy lifting in the plant, Lee looks a decade older than his fifty years. The railroad tracks that once shipped Firestone rims to keep America's tractors rolling now lead nowhere. Lee's hands are empty, restless, wanting to do something, but unable to find work. In Lee's prime, these powerful, calloused hands used to hoist eighty-pound steel tractor-wheel rims at a rate of sixty-two an hour. He worked overtime, moving from the assembly line to drive the forklift at the warehouse, coming to work on time day after day for nearly twenty years before the plant closed in August, 1982.

The management didn't announce the plant's closure date. One day, Lee came to work and the gate was locked. Six hundred workers lost their jobs, part of the 2.6 million U.S. factory workers dislocated between 1981 and 1985. When Lee's unemployment insurance ran out, he was forced to go on welfare to feed his wife and six children. Finally, after two years, he got a job at General Motors.

GM promised Lee the world, but he was laid off three days before Christmas of 1987. He was lucky to land a third factory job making car seats, but a year later he was laid off a third time. He is now on permanent unemployment and still looking for a job. The last place he applied, there were 10,000 applications for ten positions. The wages were one-third of what he'd earned at Firestone, with no health benefits, and Lee's wife has a heart condition.

"If you have a family to support, there's nothing out there," Lee says.

The riverfront mills where Lee followed his father to work no longer produce most of the steel for the American auto industry. The home where Lee raised his children has been torn down and the ethnic neighborhood condemned in order to build a waste disposal plant. The diner where he fell in love with his future wife Retha, a coal miner's daughter, has been turned into a nickel-plating factory. The steel plant where his father repaired boilers is now falling to the wrecker's ball. All but one of the two dozen factories that once lined the waterfront have been torn down.

Visiting Lee in 1991, I found the Stars and Stripes waving proudly in front of his rented, wood-frame house. The flag was displayed to honor the troops in the Persian Gulf War. Lee hoped that Americans would start buying U.S. cars again, but that same week, U.S. automakers announced a $2 billion loss.

Lee's youngest daughter, Renee, had a 3.87 grade point average in high school, but she was afraid to apply to college because she didn't know where the money to pay tuition would come from. She held up her nephew Joey, son of Lee's oldest daughter, for a family portrait. Joey's mother, a single parent, had left him with his grandparents and aunt while she looked for work. She received welfare, getting $121 every two weeks; when she got a part-time job, the state reduced benefits by more than her earnings. For one year, Joey got food supplements from Focus: HOPE, a Detroit group that feeds 80,000 families each month.

The Sliwinskis' home was pin-neat but had hardly any furniture. The family's color TV was broken for three years because it would cost $200 to fix it. For their parents' twenty-ninth anniversary, the kids got together and fixed the TV. Now Joey watches cartoons while his grandparents contemplate what happened to the American dream in Motor City, USA.

When people lose jobs, a part of them dies, the town dies around them, and death encroaches upon the city—all are threatened. What happened to Lee Sliwinski and the smokestack industries of the Rust Belt in the 1980s is now happening to skilled defense and computer workers in the Sunbelt in the 1990s. Northern California's Silicon Valley is one computer chip away from Detroit-style obsolescence; this bellwether high-tech state is in the worst slump since the Great Depression, and the end of the Cold War has provoked massive unemployment in defense industries from coast to coast. Our society is not learning from the mistakes of Detroit; it is repeating them.

That is unfortunate, because Detroit has positive lessons to teach America. After talking with Lee and other unemployed autoworkers, I discovered two hopeful programs in the Detroit area that go to great lengths to help displaced and chronically unemployed workers retrain and find new careers. The programs have different approaches. One is funded by the federal government, another privately run by a civil rights organization—but they are both effective.

The Job Connection, a Private Industry Council program funded by EDWAAA (Economic Dislocated Worker Adjustment Assistance Act) is located in the suburb of Livonia, hard hit by plant closures. Michigan law requires that plant managers notify the government sixty days before shutting down. The Job Connection swings rapidly into action, sending a team of job counselors to meet with workers at the plant before they are unemployed. Workers are given individual job counseling, including a free battery of tests to evaluate their skills and potential talents. (Sadly, Lee Sliwinski, who lives outside the Job Connection's jurisdiction, is not eligible for its services.)

Workers in the program are not isolated but create support groups helping each other cope with the transition. Psychological counselors are available to cope with the stress of job loss, which often exacerbates family problems and may trigger alcoholism and child abuse. Each worker develops a plan, with achievable goals and step-by-step actions.

The bottom line is that within weeks of getting pink slips, and before they become depressed, isolated, and despondent, workers are either in new jobs or enrolled in training programs for new careers. By minimizing the time on unemployment, the program saves taxpayer money; by investing in people's education and career planning, it creates future taxpayers.

Becky Nordstrom, a shop steward at a chemical plant that closed its doors in 1989, is an example of how the program works. Becky was among the first workers to get help from the Job Connection. The battery of tests revealed that she had management skills. Psychological counseling revealed that crippling self-doubts stemmed from childhood emotional and sexual abuse—and left her feeling worthless. Becky enrolled in college and studied business, while working part-time helping coworkers find new jobs. She quickly worked her way up to become the director of the Jobs Connection.

In the very first plant closing, the Job Connection chalked up an 89 percent success rate, either placing workers in new jobs or in job-training programs that lead toward new careers. The average cost of services is $1,500—less than a few months of unemployment insurance. "This is the mother of all Rapid Response Dislocated Worker projects," Becky says proudly. The Job Connection, one of three such experimental programs that is funded by the Department of Labor, belies the myth that the government can't help workers confronting midcareer unemployment.

Another group is Focus: HOPE, a grass-roots organization with 40,000 volunteers who pledge to take "practical action to overcome racism, poverty, and injustice." It is taking the challenge one step further by training both obsolete workers and the long-term unemployed for new jobs at the cutting edge of high technology. Founded after the 1967 Detroit riots by a Catholic priest and a middle-class housewife, Focus: HOPE is located on the twenty-three-acre site of an abandoned Ford engine plant in the heart of Detroit.

It began as a food co-op and now feeds 80,000 senior citizens, mothers, and children (at one time including Lee Sliwinski's daughter and son) each month—nearly enough people to fill the University of Michigan stadium. But cofounder Eleanor Josaitis believes that providing fish and loaves to the hungry is futile without also providing rods and teaching people how to fish.

Focus: HOPE takes hundreds of Detroiters from its food lines and trains them for jobs in the four factories it runs. To wean families from handouts, and to wean itself from government grants, the factories that manufacture pulleys, hoses, and other products are profit-making businesses that plough profits back into training people. Workers are paid a living wage and receive child care, health services, and training. The programs pay for themselves.

At its Machinist Training Institute, I met Timothy, the powerfully built Detroiter who, as a child, had watched his sister catch fire over the stove and burn to death. Timothy had survived shootings and drug pushing before fathering a family and having a crisis of conscience. He saw an advertisement for the Machinist's Institute and enrolled in the training program for computer-aided drafting and design (CADD). On his first day of class, his wife left him with their children and went to Texas. But Timothy stuck it out, learning how to use the computer terminal to design machine parts. He was competent on CADD and had nearly finished his training when I visited Focus: HOPE in 1991.

In a factory near Timothy's computer classroom, Focus: HOPE has constructed the Center for Advanced Technology, a national demonstration project. The center is training former high school dropouts and laid-off assembly line workers to become the most advanced machine-tool operaters in America. Adult students in white coats receive hands-on training while studying a full curriculum of engineering that includes courses in Japanese. Their skills are at the leading edge of technology, and their attitudes of hopeful concentration are light-years ahead of the unemployed men loitering in front of liquor stores a few blocks away. By retooling lives, Focus: HOPE is retooling American industry to become competitive again.

These programs show what can be done to help American workers survive dying industries and retrain for the future. In neighborhoods of despair, they are symbols of intelligent action and practical hope. Yet despite such successes, millions of workers like Lee Sliwinski still stand idle, waiting for retraining programs and jobs.

An even worse fate than losing a job is to lose one's health. The nightmare of middle age is to be struck down in the prime of life by a catastrophic illness without benefit of health insurance. America is the only highly industrialized democracy in the world, save South Africa, that does not have universal health coverage. For 37 million Americans without any insurance, the lack of a health-care safety net is life-threatening.

The largest group of Americans without health insurance is made up of farmers and working people employed by small businesses. Even though they may own cars and homes and have the trappings of a middle-class life-style, these hardworking, self-reliant Americans live in fear of falling ill and requiring intensive medical care. If the uninsured are lucky enough to find a hospital that will admit them without insurance, they are liable to bleed to death financially. If they survive serious illnesses such as heart disease or cancer, it is almost impossible for them to buy health insurance because "preexisting" conditions are excluded from coverage.

It is ironic that during the 1980s, the fastest-growing profit sector of the U.S. economy was the health-care "industry," while fewer and fewer Americans had access to any care at all. By the 1990s, poverty meant not only lack of money, but more critically, lack of health insurance. Medically indigent Americans are the truly poor, for their lives depend on the generosity of strangers in a strange land of cutthroat corporate medicine.

This is the story of a gentle, self-reliant man who believed in family, who made great sacrifices for his parents, and who expected that anyone who worked hard all his life and got sick had the right to health care in America.

Joe Allen Bennett, born in 1934, stayed home on the farm near Franklin, Tennessee, to care for his elderly parents. Today, Franklin isn't far by highway from the suburban outskirts of Nashville, but when Joe Allen was growing up, it seemed light-years away from the big city, close to the rural roots of the Grand Ole Opry. By Middle Tennessee standards, it wasn't much of a farm, just a little house surrounded by rocky soil—enough to grow a subsistence garden and raise a few animals for himself and his parents to be self-sufficient.

The eldest of seven children, Joe Allen used to follow in his father's footsteps, plowing the fields. He helped raise his little sisters and brothers, forestalling his own schooling so they could grow up and move on. Joe Allen never did learn how to read or write, though he could decipher the rain clouds and forecast the frost.

Farming was changing in Tennessee, and the old small acreages were no longer sufficient to support a family.

His brothers and sisters moved off to jobs, got married, and had children, but Joe Allen remained and took care of his parents. Changing bedpans, giving baths, lifting frail bodies, and preventing bedsores were duties he did with great kindness. He didn't get paid; he just did what was necessary.

When Joe Allen married, his wife came to live with him on the farm. She worked in town and, for a time, he was covered by her health insurance policy. But she suffered from lung disease, and as her health deteriorated, she had to stop working. When her company health insurance ran out, Joe Allen and his disabled wife went without coverage.

Stoically taking care of his ailing wife and his elderly parents without an outside source of income, Joe fell below the U.S. poverty line. Twenty-four million Americans—two-thirds of the nation's poor—are white families like the Bennetts. They are clustered in rural areas such as Tennessee where lack of money or insurance prevent them from gaining adequate health care.

The dry statistics don't adequately portray people like Joe Allen Bennett. In a color snapshot, he stands with his arms around his mother and father. His salt-and-pepper hair, cut short in a crewcut, frames a solid head with clear eyes. His best feature is his mouth, opening with a smile that warms the whole picture.

The photo was taken in 1983, only a few months before Joe Allen died of cancer. In his forty-ninth year, he started coughing up blood. His sister, Mattie Sue Owens, a beautician, urged him to go to a doctor. He went to a couple of country doctors who gave him cough medicine and sent him home. The bleeding got more frequent. Finally, Mattie Sue took off from work to drive him to a lung specialist. Joe Allen was scheduled for a biopsy at a modern hospital in Nashville.

"At the last minute before the lung biopsy, they did a wallet biopsy and found out he didn't have insurance," says Gordon Bonnyman, Jr., the legal aid attorney who had helped the Baskin family receive health care for their son in Nashville. Gordon recalls the Joe Allen Bennett case as one of the most tragic examples of a person falling through the cracks of the health-care system: "They canned him, demanded prepayment he didn't have. A doctor intervened and demanded emergency care."

Mattie Sue is a soft-spoken, middle-class Tennessean with the values of home and family typical of Middle America. She never had any idea that people like her brother could be turned away from health care simply because he didn't have health insurance. But in the coming months, she was to learn more than she wanted to know about barriers to health care for farmers and uninsured Americans who devote their lives to taking care of their families.

Joe Allen fell between the cracks: He was too young to be eligible for Medicare, too sick to get private insurance, too land-poor to get Medicaid. Forty-five percent of poor Americans are "too rich for Medicaid, but yet too poor for Blue Cross and Blue Shield—a very devastating problem," Dr. Harold P. Freeman said when he testified before Congress during the Bush administration. Dr. Freeman, former president of the American Cancer Society, continued: "When you add up the poor with the uninsured, it reaches the level of an estimated fifty-five million American people who are either poor or uninsured, or a combination of both."

One in five Americans. There is hardly a family without one member—a cousin, an uncle, a parent, a grandchild—who is uninsured or underinsured. Poverty is no longer defined solely by income, but by the ability to get health care without being pauperized.

The biopsy revealed Joe Allen had lung cancer. Delaying treatment even for a few days was risky; the doctor directed Joe Allen to start radiation therapy at Parkview Medical Center, the flagship of the for-profit Hospital Corporation of America in Nashville.

Mattie Sue drove her brother to the hospital and gave this version of what happened: When they reached the waiting room, Joe Allen was coughing up blood. He asked for treatment, but the hospital required $500 in cash before he could begin therapy. Joe Allen was horrified: Where would he scrape together the money? His only income was a $328 monthly Social Security check paid to his disabled wife. His parents owned the family homestead, and his only possession was a seven-year-old pickup truck.

Demanding cash up front for health care is how for-profit institutions do business. The founder of the Hospital Corporation of America, Dr. Thomas E. Frist, told me that for-profit hospitals like Parkview are not charities. They discharge their responsibility to indigent patients in two ways: First, they pay taxes. Second, they take emergency cases and stabilize patients until they can be moved to nonprofit or public institutions.

Emergency care has a strict definition, according to Gordon Bonnyman: It means being in a condition in which one is likely to suffer from loss of life, limb, or major body function if untreated in the next twenty-four hours. "If you're Joe Allen Bennett throwing up your insides, but not going to die in twenty-four hours, you have no right," Gordon says bitterly.

The family scraped together $500; radiation treatments began on a cash-as-you-go basis. Every day for thirty-five days, Joe Allen was to come for radiation. The cost of the treatments was between $35 to $75 per treatment, for a total of between $1,200 and $2,600. Midway in the treatments, Mattie Sue was stopped in the waiting room at Parkview and told to go to the business office. She went alone, to spare her brother the embarrassment and pain of seeing his health equated with cold cash. The clerk said Parkview would discontinue Joe Allen's cancer treatments, even though his life depended on them. Mattie Sue pleaded that they'd applied for Medicaid and it would almost certainly be approved.

"You're not approved yet," the clerk snapped. "This is not a charity."

Mattie Sue looked at the woman with disbelief. This was her brother who was being turned away; he was out in the lobby, sick and helpless. When she told him, Joe Allen turned away in shame and humiliation. "I'm gonna die because I don't have the money to be treated," he groaned.

Angry but not powerless, Mattie Sue called an acquaintance at the Hospital Corporation of America and pleaded for help. The executive told her he was deeply sorry, but prepayment was the principle of the corporation.

In desperation, Mattie Sue called legal aid. Gordon, who has practiced health-care law for seventeen years, listened to her story. It fell into a familiar pattern of patients being dumped by hospitals and medical corporations because they couldn't pay their bills. In his office overlooking the county courthouse, near the site where his great-great-grandfather had been the first post–Civil War governor of Tennessee, Gordon Bonnyman was waging a lonely campaign against alleged abuses of the for-profit hospitals and the not-for-profit competitors who, in his view, were just as mercenary.

His file cabinets bulged with appeals for victims. He gathered the facts in the Joe Allen Bennett case and filed a complaint in chancery court. He pleaded for the judge to grant an injunction to prevent the Hospital Corporation of America from "continuing to engage in outrageous conduct and the intentional infliction of mental distress, and to prevent the corporation's abandonment of its patient."

Faced with a court challenge, the Hospital Corporation relented, Gordon says. Joe Allen was given his treatments. Medicaid finally sent him his Medicaid card to pay for treatments.

When it became clear that the disease had progressed too far and treatments were futile, Joe Allen didn't want to go back to the hospital. He just wanted to be with his family. As he lay dying, the family gathered around. Mattie Sue sat on the side of the bed and cradled Joe Allen in her arms until he breathed his last breath.

Mattie Sue told Joe Allen's story to the press. There was a brief flurry of attention and the Hospital Corporation of America sent a $500 refund, with no explanation, no apology, nothing.

When I visited Mattie Sue in the home she and her husband built for their children, she told me that ever since Joe Allen's death, she no longer feels secure.

"I worked all my life," she said softly. "I paid into this society that refused him." Her voice breaks. "I don't think anyone realizes how vulnerable we are. . . . If you're dying, they can still say, 'No way.'"

Since Joe Allen died, the Hospital Corporation of America has become the "most profitable of the industry giants," according to a 1990 article in the *Nashville Tennessean*. Its operating profit margin increased from 16.6 percent in 1986 to 21.5 percent in 1990. Across America, for-profit hospitals are changing the face of medical care, demanding cash payments up front and denying care to the uninsured. Families struggle to get care without humiliation.

"We are just one accident or diagnosis away from being in the same boat as people in these horror stories," Gordon warns. "If you got money, you're welcome. If you don't have insurance, God have mercy on your soul and body."

As long as America lacks a system of universal health insurance, millions of critically ill Americans could find themselves in Joe Allen Bennett's shoes. Without catastrophic coverage, even insured families are one hospitalization away from losing everything, like the Millers in Indiana.

For people in middle age, the problem of diminishing access is compounded by the soaring cost of health care. Between 1987 and 1992, health expenditures in the United States nearly doubled, from $494 billion to $817 billion. The share of the gross national product spent on health escalated from 10.9 percent to 14 percent in five years, according to the U.S. Department of Commerce. In contrast, Germany spends only 8 percent of its gross national product on health care, and all citizens are covered for doctor fees and hospital costs, without deductibles.

The reasons for America's soaring health costs are complicated, but among them are high profit margins, lack of cost controls, incentives to provide expensive procedures, inadequate focus on prevention, overinvestment in high technology, monumental waste and inefficiency, duplicative procedures, voluminous paperwork, defensive medicine resulting from threats of malpractice suits, and the vain hope that somehow death can be forestalled by just spending more money.

President Bill Clinton has made health insurance a priority of his administration, asking First Lady Hillary Rodham Clinton to lead the effort to draft a consensus health-reform package. But, as of this writing, there is no clear consensus on what legislation will finally emerge from Capitol Hill and be signed into law. Differences between "managed-competition," employer-sponsored, and government-run proposals are hard for average Americans to evaluate.

Americans now seem to agree that the bottom line is to control health-care costs and extend comprehensive health coverage to every American. Middle-aged Americans must not be denied timely treatment, as Joe Allen Bennett was—or be left with America's wasteful $800-billion-a-year health bill.

A third major and predictable crisis of middle age is taking responsibility for an aging parent, sick spouse, or crippled child—or all of the above. The burden of being sandwiched between the vulnerabilities of children and the frailties of old age usually falls on women. Working women are asked not only to be part-time or full-time workers, but to be dutiful mothers, wives, and daughters. The breakdown of families makes it all the more necessary to have stable support institutions—child care, elder care, home care. But these community services are overwhelmed and starved for government support.

Jean Comer, the director of Options for Recovery, the drug treatment program that helped Kenya Williams deliver a clean baby, is one professional woman who was confronted with the mid-life conflict between the demands of her job and the burden of illness in her family.

Jean's mother, Harriet Houston, began suffering the final stages of emphysema just when Kenya's son Miles was being born. A divorcée who had supported herself for years in the family funeral business, Harriet now needed an oxygen tank to breathe. She wanted to remain in her own home, but she needed a caretaker to be with her twenty-four hours a day. Harriet's medical bills were paid by Medicare and she had sufficient outside income to obtain some hired help. Jean's daughter and nephew pitched in by living part-time with their beloved grandmother. But the responsibility for weaving all these tenuous arrangements into a web of care fell squarely on Jean's shoulders.

The sudden physical vulnerability of Harriet, who had always been self-reliant, opened up Jean's own emotional vulnerability. She wanted to be with her dying mother, to gather the colorful stories of her mother's childhood as a girl orphaned by tuberculosis in Colorado. Yet Jean wanted to move forward with her own life after having just sent the last of her children off to college.

She was devoted to her clients at Options for Recovery, but in facing this family crisis she found she had few options of her own. The ten-hour workdays coping with women in recovery, coupled with hourlong commutes to her mother's home in Chula Vista, California, left her ragged. The drug treatment program had no family-leave provision for employees to take off for a few weeks or months to care for sick children or dying parents. Jean was forced to choose between being on call to answer the piercing screams of mothers in recovery or to hear the paper-thin wheeze of her mother sucking oxygen from a respirator in her bedroom.

Jean finally made the agonizing choice to leave Options and help her mother breathe more comfortably at home for as long as possible. This meant temporarily sacrificing her salary; it also meant the potential loss of Social Security benefits when Jean reached retirement age.

Because America does not require small business* to provide family leave, and because the Social Security sys-

---

* Large corporations are now required to provide short-term family leave.

tem does not acknowledge the contributions of Americans who assume caretaking roles, women like Jean Comer are put in triple jeopardy for helping their families. Their work is interrupted, their income is cut, and their pensions are reduced.

Helping one's own mother is as hard, or harder, than providing professional treatment to drug mothers, Jean confided to me. When I visited Harriet at home, the bright yellow house overlooking a canyon near the Mexican border was filled with sunlight as Harriet told stories of her impoverished childhood in Colorado.

There is a haunting continuity in the lives of families: One hard-luck generation gets help; the next, more fortunate generation helps others. In 1921, when Harriet was five, her mother died of tuberculosis. Her destitute father, who had lost his farm, put his children in an orphanage for TB victims' families. The Colorado Springs Day Nursery gave Harriet an education and the opportunity for a better life, which she passed on to her daughter Jean, who went to college and became relatively well-off. Today's hard-luck children are threatened by new epidemics of crack and AIDS. At Options, Jean created a haven for drug mothers and babies. She calls it a "payback," a commitment to helping others that she learned from her mother.

Midsentence, Harriet begins to cough. Her daughter quietly comes to her aid, gently holding her mother as she was once cradled as a baby. When the roles of mother and daughter are reversed, it causes emotional turmoil for everyone. Being with her mother offers Jean a way, in these precious hours, to give back to her all she has given over a lifetime.

When Jean leaves her mother's bedside in the evening, she is physically and emotionally spent. Yet she still has the duties of a wife and mother to perform, and the unfulfilled need to contribute and be valued through her work. Mid-life is the backbone of the life span, supporting young and old on its shoulders. When the strain gets too great and the backbone buckles under, all generations are threatened. On such weary days, when ordinary Americans struggle to fulfill their obligations without a railing to lean on, the middle of the journey seems endless.

RETIREMENT, AGING, AND DYING

LIVING IS FOR THE ELDERLY

Aging in America is a frayed patchwork quilt of golden age condos and lonely retirement hotels. Walled off within exclusive, gated communities from their poorer neighbors, the wealthiest retirees are living high at the expense of their indebted country, receiving subsidized health care and pensions millionaires don't need, while lobbying for tax cuts. Meanwhile, in single rooms in decaying urban neighborhoods, the poorest widows in their eighties are eking out their days on tiny pensions, unable to pay for medicines, afraid to walk out on the street.

Most of America's 4 to 7 million impoverished seniors, depending on whose poverty figures you use, are women. Women live longer than men do, and over their lifetimes, women have suffered gender discrimination in family roles, employment, and Social Security. The Older Women's League warns today's working women that unless changes are made in wage and pension systems, they will follow the footsteps of their widowed grandmothers into poverty.

Most of America's 30 million retirees, however, are better off than previous generations of senior citizens. The relative wealth of Americans who grew up in the Great Depression and fought in World War II is, of course, the result of hard work, sacrifice, and luck. But it is also due to a lifetime of government subsidies, beginning with the New Deal, continuing through the GI Bill, accelerating with Great Society entitlements, and culminating in the Reagan tax cuts.

This is a retirement story not of one person, but of a generation. It is told impersonally, because its intention is not to cast a shadow on any individual, but to shed light on the cumulative effects of policies that benefited seniors at the expense of their less-fortunate peers and young people.

When Michael Harrington investigated poverty in the early 1960s, he discovered that the elderly were among the poorest, most neglected, and most deprived citizens living in "The Other America." The outrage against elder poverty led to Great Society programs like Medicare and Medicaid, to exponential increases in Social Security benefits, and a host of special programs and tax incentives for seniors.

The result of this massive social investment in the elderly was spectacularly successful. In 1959, the poverty rate for the elderly was twice that of children. Today, seniors have half the poverty rate of children.

The hidden cost of middle-class entitlement programs for the elderly put a larger burden on working people. The Social Security Act of 1935 was established as a "compact" between generations, but it favors the old over the young. In 1950, seventeen workers were employed for every person receiving Social Security benefits. Today, the ratio is three workers per retiree. When Baby Boomers retire in the next century, the ratio will slip to two workers per pensioner.

Today's working people are paying excess payroll taxes to fund benefits for today's pensioners. The annual surplus being paid into Social Security is $56 billion. Its ostensible purpose is to provide for the needs of Baby Boomers once they retire. Actually, this surplus is also being used to ease the federal budget deficit, and to make the national debt look smaller than it really is. Baby Boomers question whether their generation will receive the benefits to which they are entitled, or whether the government will loot Social Security in order to pay off its bad debts.

One solution, advocated by economist Milton Friedman, is to dismantle Social Security step-by-step, honoring today's commitments to today's pensioners but gradually phasing out the public system and encouraging free-market pensions. An overwhelming majority of Americans oppose such radical action. Without Social Security, many seniors would slip slowly into poverty, while a few became tycoons.

A better solution is to preserve Social Security and, to offset its negative effects on working families, create a public trust fund for children. Such a fund, which will be outlined in the last chapter, would support reliable services for children and families. It would complement Social Security and fulfill the compact between generations.

But the difficulty of convincing seniors to pay higher taxes to provide a legacy for children is exemplified by the tragic fate of a similar attempt to improve the Medicare system: In 1988, Congress passed the Medicare Catastrophic Coverage Act, and President Reagan signed it into law. This provided supplemental insurance so that expenses not covered by Medicare did not force seniors with catastrophic medical bills into poverty. The money was to be raised through a supplemental premium, or surtax, on Medicare benefits. In effect, it pooled money from all seniors to help those who faced catastrophic medical expenses not covered by Medicare. But vocal seniors who didn't want to pay for their less-well-off peers lobbied Congress, and the law was repealed the following year, 1989.

As a group, today's retirees are the wealthiest retired Americans in this country's history. They have received more government benefits than any generation before or since. Their median income is twice as high as the average working family's, and their taxes are far lower than other age groups'. Their willingness to heed President Clinton's call for sacrifice to reduce the deficit could have a lasting effect on the future of their children, grandchildren, and of coming generations.

At some indefinable point, people pass from the vitality of work to the fragility of old age and retirement. The stairs that seemingly led upward, stage after stage, reverse direction, leading downward to decline. The inevitable tragedy of aging is loss. The toll takes so many forms— loss of health, loved ones, financial security, and independence. The most crippling losses take away the will to live.

Americans have an especially hard time growing old, because our culture equates dependency with failure. The pervasive fear of elderly Americans is of losing their independence, of having to rely on others to house, feed, and clothe them.

At Unquity House, an attractive residence for the elderly in a suburb of Boston, there is a way for older people to make the gradual transition from independence to partial dependence with dignity. They are able to proceed rapidly or slowly, according to their own needs and fortunes. People in their sixties who still work live in apartments next to those in their eighties who require assistance and care. The state of Massachusetts helped build the high-rise building, whose windows overlook woods. Residents describe it as a pleasant and safe place to live. Various agencies provide transportation, health services, and recreation. The key is to help people remain semi-independent as long as possible. Due to a shortage of units, however, there is a long waiting list of seniors wishing to move into Unquity House—a problem common to many parts of the country.

As in every place where Americans grow old, residents of Unquity House live in dire fear of losing their last shred of self-reliance—having a stroke, or breaking a hip—and being put in a nursing home. Old people who are sick and in pain will do almost anything to hide their frailty so they won't be taken from their homes and put away in institutions. In America, the punishment for getting old is to have one's life prolonged, while the conditions of existence torture the spirit within. Our government will pay for people to be put away in nursing homes, but it will not help relatives take care of them at home.

Massachusetts has been a national pioneer in providing services for the elderly. One winter day, I followed a home-care worker on his rounds from apartment to row house in East Boston. With the help of a visiting nurse, a retired baggage handler named Antonio was taking care of his stroke-paralyzed wife at home. Tough-talking to outsiders but gentle with his family, Antonio revealed his strength through a determination to perform domestic chores with uncomplaining kindness. Day and night, he turned his wife in bed to prevent bedsores, emptied bedpans, gave her medications, cooked, cleaned, and babysat for his grandchild while his daughter was working. No saint, he merely said that his wife had always taken care of him; now it was his turn. The federal government wouldn't help Antonio take care of her at home, although Medicaid would pay for her to go into a nursing home.

But the state of Massachusetts saw the human value—and the financial benefits—of helping people take care of their own at home. It provided up to $4,000 of respite care a year—home-nursing visits, cleaning, and transportation—to assist family caregivers like Antonio.

Most states do not provide sufficient funding for home care. Each year, thousands of elderly Americans are put into institutions because Medicaid automatically pays nursing homes but only rarely reimburses home care. On any given day, 10 million Americans are caring for a sick, elderly family member at home. Providing home assistance would cost an estimated $12 billion a year, but proponents say it would reduce suffering and save billions spent unnecessarily on nursing homes.

The philosophy behind home health care is that it benefits all parties: the patient, the caregiver, and the state. Most elderly patients prefer to remain at home for as long as possible. Devoted friends and family members will make great sacrifices for their loved ones, yet elderly people cannot do this difficult work alone without endangering their own health and well-being. They need professional assistance, supplies, transportation, and spells of relief to keep up with their own lives. Although these home visits are costly, they are usually far less expensive than twenty-four-hour care in an institution.

Clearly, some people need the full-time care available in nursing homes. On any given day, 1.5 million Americans are confined to nursing homes. America spends $30 billion annually on their care: Half comes from private sources, and half from the government.

Inhumane conditions in some homes are periodically spotlighted by federal and state inquiries that show everything from neglect to filth to overmedication. As a young editorial writer in San Diego, I was shocked by the conditions in a county-run nursing home, and editorial-ized to clean it up or shut it down. The federal government withheld Medicaid funding until the institution passed inspections. But over the past twelve years, federal inspections of nursing homes have lapsed and abuses have gone unreported or unchallenged. Business interests have been more successful in lobbying Washington for tax breaks than nursing home rights groups have been in protecting old people who can't fend for themselves.

Even in the best nursing homes, life is difficult, especially for people who are fully conscious but emotionally cut off from family and home. Periodically, outsiders have crusaded for better conditions, but the most courageous activists are residents who struggle for rights and dignity within the walls of nursing homes.

Assistance that lets the elderly help themselves is as crucial at this season of life as in youth and middle age. Many of the same techniques that help younger people— from support groups to art therapy—have been adapted to help the elderly cope. Participation, expression, and involvement in decision making are life-affirming as opposed to merely life-preserving, and enhance the quality and meaning of existence.

Christina Halkett is one such fighter. A spry ninety-two-year-old widow, she suffered a paralyzing stroke in 1976. Hospitalized and pauperized by medical expenses, physically unable to live alone, Christina has been confined to a nursing home for fifteen years. Her tenacious struggle shows that even in the most alienating circumstances, life can be sustained through courage and the support of others.

In the depths of the Bostonian Nursing Care Center in Dorchester, Massachusetts, Christina clings steadfastly to life with her blue-veined fingers. As winter's light falls on her lively face, translucent as a portrait by Vermeer, her spirit shows through the wrinkles of age.

When Christina was brought into this netherworld at age seventy-eight, she was recovering from a stroke that paralyzed her from the neck down. For this woman born in Scotland at the turn of the century—a bonny lass who began work at thirteen, immigrated to America, and was a union garment worker for twenty-seven years—it was like entering a tomb.

She was still partially paralyzed and unable to fend for herself when she was transported from the hospital to the forbidding brick nursing home. Describing those first days fifteen years later, Christina says she knew not a soul, and no one introduced her to the other residents. A pall of silence hung over the institution, as if there were an unspoken agreement not to communicate. When she entered the room of a neighbor, hoping to strike up a conversation, she remembers being told by a staffer to get out. The doctors and nurses seemed to treat patients as if they didn't have a mind of their own.

The smell of decay and disinfectant permeated the building, isolated from the social life of the surrounding working-class neighborhood. Within the institution's walls, wheelchairs were gridlocked in corridors, their lonely occupants stalled on life's journey, unable to reach their final destination or to turn back. Crippled in body, but her Scottish spirit hungering to live, Christina felt confined to a living death.

At mealtime, Christina expected the silence to be broken and people to take bread in communion, talking and laughing. But when she entered the antiseptic dining room for the first time, she was stunned by the silence of the diners. Around her the ghostlike people ate without so much as looking at each other.

Struggling with all her might to control her half-paralyzed limbs, Christina gripped the edge of the table and pulled herself up to her full five-foot, one-inch height. Holding on to the back of her chair for dear life, she addressed her fellow residents: "Isn't this supposed to be a home and we're all here together?"

A cafeteria worker hissed for her to let the people dine in peace. But Christina held her ground. "This is the one place where we all can meet!" she cried in a trembling voice. As all eyes turned to this birdlike woman with blue eyes aglow, she pleaded for people to stop ignoring each other and converse as friends did on the outside, asking how each other was, where they came from. She raised a *cri de coeur* against the code of silence: "This is our home and we should be allowed to talk at mealtime."

Since that day, Christina has refused to be silenced, and her lilting voice speaking up for the rights of nursing home residents has been heard all the way to the governor's office. She thought her life was finished, but realized it was just beginning.

A seamstress, Christina was determined to regain the use of her hands. With the help of a machine to strengthen dexterity, she practiced and practiced until she was able to thread a needle. When she was barely able to walk, she clutched the walls of the corridor and made the rounds to her neighbors' rooms, knocking on doors until she was welcome. Slowly she helped break down the walls of isolation. She had to fight the system of inertia and despair to do it.

Christina found crucial allies in her struggle when she heard about a meeting of a group called LIFE. Curious, she attended the get-together and learned that LIFE stood for Living Is for the Elderly. The self-help organization was made up of hundreds of nursing home residents like herself; its purpose was to organize and lobby for people who lived in nursing homes scattered around the

Boston area. She took an instant liking to the founder of LIFE, Ed Alessi. He was not a senior citizen, but a middle-aged social worker who worked with military veterans in nursing homes. Ed wasn't content to work solely as a social worker; he identified with the elderly's suffering and was disturbed by the powerlessness of these once-vigorous men and women. He believed that it was crucial for them to band together to fight for their own rights.

After work, evenings and weekends, with no remuneration for himself, Ed began building a volunteer organization of nursing home residents. He likened their struggle for basic rights to the civil rights movement. He could not agitate for them; they would have to advocate for their own needs. But if they were confined to institutions, he could establish communication between them, and he could provide transportation to government offices and the State House hearings.

"The elderly experience the same thing as other minorities," Ed told me on a visit with Christina and other LIFE members, as he careened through wintry South Boston from nursing home to nursing home. "It's a difficult group to organize because no one admits they're old."

The purpose of the grass-roots organization, funded on a shoestring budget, was to help nursing home residents become agents of change. Legislators ignored the pleas of frustrated social workers like Ed, but they listened when Christina and other nursing home residents spoke up about their problems and needs.

LIFE members regularly testify in state hearings, lobby politicians, and suggest changes in nursing home rules that permit residents greater control over decisions. LIFE campaigned for and won a modest increase in the personal allowances that nursing home residents received. Elder activists have made Massachusetts a national leader in its treatment of the elderly.

But when I visited Boston in 1991, the Northeast was leading the nation in the recession, and the state was reducing services and allowances. Kit Watson, ninety-nine years old, wanted to send a present to the boys in the Persian Gulf, but her $72.80 Medicaid allowance had been cut to $60 and Ed feared it would be reduced to $30. For people like Kit who worked all their lives and were forced to become paupers to qualify for Medicaid, the allowance is the only income they have left in the world.

"She wants control in her life," Ed says. "Before, she was independent. Now she has to ask for permission to do anything. It's not as if they're born in a nursing home," he sighs. "But that's how they're treated."

Her plight mirrors that of children, as funding for services declines across the board. The humanization of the elder-care system today is in the long-term interest of people who will need it tomorrow. Baby Boomers are only preparing the bed they will lie in.

Christina sits beside her bed, maintaining hope within the gloom. Quietly she speaks of her roommate, who moans and wanders out of the room with the dementia of Alzheimer's. The pitiful woman often doesn't know where she is. When she wanders back into the room, Christina takes the woman in her arms and cradles her like a baby and mothers her. "Baby, I've been waiting for you."

This is Christina's purpose in life. To alleviate pain. To connect through the woman's skin to her heart. To adopt the orphans of age. To make the nursing facility a loving home. "There isn't one in here who I can't feel sorry for," she says without a trace of self-pity.

Christina's world is small: one-half of a 150-square-foot room containing a bed, a wooden dresser, a window greened by potted plants, and a carton of newsletters testifying to fifteen years of activism. She is confined with a roommate who no longer remembers her name, but

Christina knows the name of everyone on her corridor and is connected to a network of friends who have become her second family. She is no longer paralyzed, physically or politically, and her buoyant voice is fearless and strong. "Show kindness and you get it back," she says.

Facing death is the final challenge for everyone. The ultimate struggle to find meaning and make peace with one's life is complicated by what literary critic Robert Pinsky calls "the effort to keep death as it once was—a phenomenon of one's particular human body and soul—and to prevent it from becoming altogether a phenomenon of health care." The traditional rituals of death have been supplanted by "the new landscape of death," Pinsky writes. "Here, the old intimation of mortality has yielded to the second opinion. The last words, the blessing of the young, the washing of the body, the coins in the eyelids, the deathbed confession, the deathbed reconciliation, and the deathbed farewell have been succeeded or crowded out by the IV, the respirator, the feeding tubes in the nostrils, the living will, the hospital roommate, the nurses."

The phenomenon of terminal health care is immensely costly in suffering and in dollars. Former Surgeon General C. Everett Koop estimates that 80 percent of the money a person spends over a lifetime on medical services is expended in the last six months of life.

This lopsided percentage can be explained by several factors: First, fatal illnesses are the most severe, and aggressive treatment is costly. Second, doctors are "not in the business of helping people die," says one physician who has practiced medicine for forty years. Doctors are trained to be proactive, not passive, and they tend to view terminal illness as potentially curable and each patient's death as a personal defeat. Third, families feel guilty for letting loved ones die without doing everything possible for them. Fourth, medical care is a business that earns a percentage of profit from treatment: Generally, the higher the volume of care, the more earned. Fifth, people who are terminally ill may make "advance directives" about what procedures they do not wish to be performed, but these living wills are controversial and sometimes ignored. Finally, despite the growing use of hospice care, allowing terminally ill patients to die at home surrounded by their families, most Americans do not receive cost-effective palliative care. Instead, they die in hospitals—at great cost in dollars and suffering.

Consumer Reports magazine calculated in 1992 that of the $800 billion-plus health bill America pays each year, $200 billion was wasted in unnecessary, overpriced, and useless medical expenditures, or through inefficient bureaucracy and overhead. That same year, Medicare benefits alone for 35 million senior citizens totaled $129 billion.

According to a 1984 study by the Health Care Finance Administration, 28 percent of all Medicare expenditures in any one year are spent on elderly patients during their last twelve months of life. Thirty percent of that amount is spent in the last month of life. Therefore, it can be estimated that in 1991, the federal government spent $36 billion for Medicare for elderly people in their last year of life—$11 billion in the final month.

To get a relative comparison of costs and priorities, the federal government spent nearly twice as much on Medicare for elderly people in their *final month* of life as it did on Medicaid for children in their *first twenty years of life*. Medicare is only a fraction of the total spending for the terminally ill elderly, but the immense disparity between

$36 billion for Medicare in the final year of life and roughly $8 billion on Medicaid for children under twenty-one reveals a tragic imbalance in the nation's priorities.*

Medicare spending has increased twentyfold since its inception in 1965. At the same time, access to free or subsidized health services for children has been curtailed by cuts at every level of government.

Hospice care is a humane, cost-effective alternative to wasteful hospital care for the dying. In the early 1980s, Congress authorized studies of hospice care. They revealed that palliative care for terminally ill people expiring at home or in a hospice was significantly less costly—in dollars and in the agony of dying—than hospital care for terminal patients.

In 1984, Medicare began providing hospice benefits. For that first year, there were 2,200 hospice admissions, and by 1991, more than 112,000 people received federally funded hospice-care reimbursements. That year, Medicare spent $465 million on hospice benefits—only *one-twentieth* of the total Medicare spending for people in their last month of life. The average hospice stay was fifty-three days, and the average Medicare reimbursement was about $5,000 per patient. In a hospital, $5,000 would be spent in three days; a fifty-three-day hospital stay would cost upward of $100,000.

The cost of hospitalizing the terminally ill is significantly higher than the maximum amount reimbursed by Medicare. A 1992 study in Buffalo, New York, averaged

* The imbalance in federal health-care spending between the elderly and children is mind-boggling. In 1990, the federal government spent $6.9 billion on Medicaid for poor children and $1.2 billion on "medically needy" children (like A.J. Miller), for a total of $8.3 billion on all children. Children receive only 12.5 percent of Medicaid's budget, in comparison to 27 percent of the budget that goes to the elderly. In addition, all elderly Americans are entitled to Medicare, but no children are eligible. In 1990, the total Medicare budget was $107 billion—about thirteen times the Medicaid budget for poor children and 100 times the amount for medically needy children.

the bills of seventeen terminal patients who were eligible for hospice care, but were treated in a hospital instead. These patients had a prognosis of six months or less to live, and standard procedures indicated that they should receive palliative treatment of life-limiting diseases.

The study revealed that the hospital lost nearly $12,000 per patient for services that were not reimbursed by Medicare. The study also estimated that $2.4 million was lost annually by this single hospital for treating terminal patients who would be better cared for at home or in a hospice setting.

Nationally, billions of dollars are lost by hospitals treating terminal patients who are unable to benefit from intensive hospital care and require palliative hospice care. These losses are shifted in bookkeeping and are ultimately borne by other patients, their insurance companies, and the taxpayers.

More important than the waste of billions of dollars is the toll of suffering inflicted on terminal patients and their families by hospital procedures that do little to extend life, but make its culminating experience a nightmare of pain, isolation, confusion, and horror. Even more beneficial than the saving of health dollars is the human benefit of the hospice alternative, which allows terminally ill people to make choices regarding their bodies, their treatment, the place of their dying, and the people with whom they spend their last moments.

The philosophy of hospice is that death, for the terminally ill, is a natural part of life, not a disease to be fought indefinitely. The process of dying is honored by helping people go through this final passage with dignity, in a homelike setting, in the company of friends and loved ones. Emphasis is placed on the alleviation of suffering: Hospice does not mean passively standing by while a person goes through the agony of dying; it uses aggressive measures to deal with pain, including the choice of receiving narcotic medications that would not be appropriate for people with nonterminal illnesses. Unlike hospital care that focuses on the ill patient, the family is considered the unit of care in a hospice. A team of caregivers makes available services to meet the physical, psychological, social, and spiritual needs of the patient and the family.

Hospice care is not appropriate for many people, nor should anyone be forced to receive it. Legally, there are two basic guidelines for eligibility: (1) A physician must certify that nothing more can be done curatively, and (2) the patient has less than six months to live.

A national association of hospice organizations estimates that between 60 and 70 percent of terminally ill patients would be eligible for hospice care, but less than half of them use it. There are only 1,900 hospice facilities in the United States, and many people live too far away from one to receive care.

Fear, guilt, and ignorance are factors preventing more people from availing themselves of hospice care. Yet it is an option taken by a growing number of Americans who wish to live a full life and die with a measure of control, contact, and consciousness—and be spared a living death on respirators, heart pumps, and IVs.

There is no single way to die well, any more than there is a single model for going through adolescence or middle age. Veteran hospice workers speak of the transforming effect that imminent death has not only on the patient, but on the entire family. There are opportunities to ask for forgiveness and forgive others; to comfort and be comforted; to reappraise one's life and to receive praise for it;

to anguish and to resolve; to lose control and to gain meaning.

Comforting the dying helps diminish the fear of mortality that contorts our culture and distorts our priorities. The hospice movement can help America face death with compassion and renew its birthright.

The end of the journey dovetails with the beginning, as the hard choices of dying mirror those surrounding birth.

The drama of death and birth is played out daily on a hilltop in San Diego, where a public hospital overlooks Mission Valley. At the University of California San Diego Medical Center one New Year's Day, an old man died and twin girls were born. The old man had waited 100 days for death and had been kept alive on machines; the girls received no prenatal care and arrived 90 days premature.

The man had entered the hospital with severe burns to the bottom of both feet. A diabetic, legally blind, and partially deaf, he had lost sensation in his feet and didn't know how he had burned them. The burn unit attempted to treat the burns, but the infection had gone too far. Both legs were amputated. When he realized he had no legs, he became depressed. He withdrew and stopped fighting.

But his body didn't quit. He had pneumonia, he could not breathe without a respirator, he suffered poor nutrition, and he was exhausted. Each of these conditions was potentially reversible, but together, they gave him little chance of recovering.

Lifting him was like taking a piece of meat out of bed and putting it in a chair, according to one nurse who found his agony wrenching. The man stared off into space. When he finally died, he looked like "a little puppy—he just gave up," she said. Describing the ordeal, the young nurse's face showed the strain of working in an intensive care unit where 40 percent of her patients die—many after being kept alive by heroic measures, when they want to die.

"We've put a lot of people through hell," she said. "When people are asked if they want everything done to save them, they need to know what everything is like." It means choking on the respirator; alarms going off every ten minutes; getting stuck with needles; tubes in every orifice; rib-cracking heart resuscitation; no sleep; pain, confusion, and delirium. Her coworker said everyone over the age of seventy should be taken to an intensive care unit and shown the people with tubes and respirators. Then they should be given a chance to sign a right-to-die form.

The old man, a former naval intelligence officer, didn't sign the form, according to hospital records. He knew he was getting on, the nurse said. A few years before, he had sold his coin collection and taken a trip around the world. Then he came back to San Diego for the last time.

He died on his 100th day in the intensive care unit. The bill to Medicare was $326,312. The man's anguish was incalculable.

On the day that he died, a nineteen-year-old woman gave birth to twins. The joy of new life was dampened by the fact that the babies, who had received no prenatal care, were three months premature and at risk of dying or being permanently disabled.

"She's a high-risk mother, and she knew it," said a nurse. She was also a teenager, with no husband and two previous miscarriages. She had given birth to another premature baby boy in January who was hospitalized for six and a half months. Soon after going home, the baby took sick and was rushed back to the hospital, where he died. His treatment cost Medi-Cal, California's Medicaid agency, $393,580.

This was a classic case of why children need prenatal care, said a doctor who treated the baby. He was disturbed that after all this, the mother didn't receive prenatal care for her next pregnancy. She said she called for an appointment at an overwhelmed and underfunded community clinic and was told that the first available slot was for a month later. It was too late. She showed up for her first prenatal visit with contractions, in the second trimester. Then she discovered she was bearing twins.

The tiny girls were isolated in the intensive care unit. Their legs were as long as fountain pens, their fingers the size of paper clips. The doctor said they were doing remarkably well and they would remain in the hospital until their due date in about three months. At $1,500 a day for each child, the Medi-Cal bill reached $270,000.

That is a high price to pay for the lack of prenatal care. The teenage mother refused to admit she was pregnant until it was too late, and the clinic failed to respond, also too late. Denial is a common response of teenage mothers facing pregnancy and of old people facing terminal diseases. It is also a symptom—and a result—of our dysfunctional insurance and health-care systems, which routinely fail to respond to the needs of pregnant mothers and terminally ill patients. We hide from the possibility of death and deny the need for prenatal care. As a result of such systematic failures in health care, the hospital bills for the old man and the young mother's three children would total $1 million.

These cases are tragically routine. In the same intensive care ward with the old man, six other patients lay dying—at great suffering and incredible expense. The twins were among hundreds of "no-care" babies born annually at this hospital and consuming millions of dollars of intensive care.*

Such tragic waste of lives makes it seem that there is no mercy for the dying, no hope for babies. But America also provides better options for treating both the terminally ill and the newborn. Recently, a new birth center and hospice were built on the hillcrest above San Diego. Poor mothers who have received prenatal care now routinely deliver healthy babies at the Birth Place, just footsteps from the hospital where Kenya Williams's firstborn crack baby died. Within view of the intensive care unit where the old man expired, a privately funded hospice has rooms with big picture windows where the dying and their families view the sun setting over the Pacific Ocean.

If the twins were born today, they would have a better chance because of improved access to prenatal care. If the old man were dying today, he would have the choice of entering a hospice and receiving help to pass away in peace.

* A version of this hospital story originally appeared in 1987 as an editorial in the *San Diego Tribune*, entitled "The Right to Prenatal Care and the Right to Die."

LIFE SPAN

WHERE THEY ARE NOW

If writing this book has convinced me of anything, it is that America needs to build a railing from nativity to old age. A support system can't remove the dangers from life, nor can it abolish poverty; but it can prevent people from having to fall all the way down the stairs before they get help. It is the bridge between our endangered present and a supportive future.

Americans now know that the old "safety net" has been dismantled from the top down. But few are aware that the railing is already being built, piece by piece, from the bottom up. The people whose lives inform this book show that Americans have the expertise to build a practical railing, if only we dedicate ourselves to complete it.

The railing is not a welfare state, where all functions are provided by the government. Nor is it a substitute for individual self-reliance or family responsibility. The railing is composed of all elements of American society: the private sector, the government, local communities, families, and individuals.

A cohesive support structure capable of sustaining Americans of all generations must:

1. Provide children with a healthy start in life.
2. Support children's development to maturity through programs in neighborhoods and schools.

3. Buttress families to protect people who depend on them.
4. Create a secure system of child support to prevent divorce from hurling children and single parents into poverty.
5. Provide a minimum level of health insurance for all Americans.
6. Offer job training for dislocated workers and counseling for people who suffer life crises.
7. Shore up the Social Security system for future generations and stop gender discrimination among pensioners.
8. Eliminate wasteful spending on futile treatments for patients in the final stages of illness and recycle health funding back to the beginning of life.
9. Make the social compact between generations a two-way street and encourage the elderly to pass on an inheritance to America's children.

People—as individuals, families, and communities—play the leading role in helping each other ascend the stairs, but the government must play a more active supporting role in four areas: child development, family support, health care, and Social Security. Ultimately, the railing would comprise an intricate network of private and public relationships that nurture and protect development, instead of thwarting it.

In hard times, more Americans may see the need for such a railing, but the problems posed by the federal deficit make it seem impossible to find the wherewithal to build one. Is this railing affordable? Yes, for two good reasons: First, the long-term costs of not having one is far more expensive and destructive than the short-term costs of building it. Second, it doesn't all have to be done at once. Erecting it piece by piece is affordable, as witnessed by the low-cost, high-yield programs profiled in this book.

The deficit does not mean America, the richest nation on earth, lacks wealth. Instead, it lacks a vision of how to spend and save—to allocate its resources wisely. Further, we lack the faith that tax revenues will be wisely spent; hence we lack the commitment to spend a sufficient proportion of our gross national product healing our grievous domestic suffering. Outwardly strong and brash, America inwardly lacks confidence in its ability to solve its domestic problems. This only prevents us from taking action, and the problems grow worse.

The Great Depression of the 1930s was more immediately threatening to Americans than the recession of the 1990s, but the psychological depression of our time is more crippling. In the 1930s, Americans believed that they could make changes to save their families and country. At the end of the American Century, many have lost confidence that this is possible. This lack of faith in ourselves as a country is reflected in our distrust of government, our fear of one another, and our blaming poor scapegoats for our problems. To get out of this crippling, depressive condition, disillusioned Americans need to jettison some destructive illusions:

- The illusion that we're poor and can't afford the basic public functions such as education, health, and child welfare.
- The illusion that we can't help people—and its mistaken corollary that trying to help people only hurts them.
- The illusion that we can become more competitive by making deeper cuts in our social infrastructure.
- The illusion that our country is unable to deal effectively with its problems. This is the most crippling of all.

- The illusion that we spend too much of our gross national product on welfare, and that recipients are living high.*
- The illusion that paying taxes is worse than paying interest on the debt. At least when ordinary Americans pay taxes, they have a chance of receiving government services. But when the government pays billions of dollars in interest on the debt, taxpayers get nothing—or worse, they pay Japan to loan to the United States.

These illusions heighten the increasingly polarized debate over poverty and social policy. Liberals believe poverty can be alleviated by spending money, without paying sufficient attention to personal responsibility. Conservatives believe that poverty can be reduced by punishing people who seek help and forcing them to become self-reliant.

The life-span approach outlined in this book sees that personal and social responsibility build on one another. It looks at people's assets as well as their needs, and directs assistance to life's transitions when people are most vulnerable and help is most effective. It differentiates between transitional dependency (of children and ailing old people) and permanent dependency (welfare for the poor and the rich). It shows how helping people develop skills may enable dependent people to achieve autonomy. It seeks to build a triangle of interdependence among individuals, families, and generations.

---

* In fact, we spend a fraction of one percent of our gross national product on Aid to Families with Dependent Children. Welfare payments are so low that they raise only 17 percent of recipients above the poverty line—half the percentage a decade before. Across the board, social spending in the United States falls far behind that of our Western European allies, and it is less effective in bringing people out of poverty. This is one reason why America has more wealth and jobs than our Western allies but a far higher percentage of families living in poverty.

A developmental approach to helping people allocates resources early in life on the assumption that prevention can reduce problems later on. It sees people unfolding, not static. It returns to the traditional notion that the role of institutions is to help people pass through the milestones of life. As families grow diffuse, a greater share of responsibility for raising children falls on institutions such as schools. They must perform their traditional academic function while also addressing the emotional and physical needs of children who come to school hungry, neglected, or abused.

This does not mean that the public institutions supplant the family, but that they provide basic services, like child care and health clinics, that families need in order to fulfill their function. When families fail to provide for children, society must take seriously its *in loco parentis* role.

Underlying this approach is the basic connection between people who share life's journey. While each individual is unique, the stages of human development are universal. All people share the vulnerability as they pass through the difficult transitions of infancy, childhood, adolescence, adulthood, mid-life, aging, and dying. At one time or another, every person needs help along the way.

Today, fearful and angry Americans are reluctant to share a park bench, much less life's journey. Racial and ethnic conflicts are tearing apart our neighborhoods, our schools, our social fabric. Whites don't want to pay for public schools and social services, because they don't feel connected to people of color, and vice versa. As old ties disintegrate, our survival depends on finding a common denominator that unites us in a new community. These stories show that the pathways out of poverty are common to all people, as basic as the steps of human development.

The value of a railing is that it helps everyone—a crack addict like Kenya Williams, and a mother with a sick baby like Cindy Miller. It is as crucial for an unemployed steelworker as for a sick farmer.

The railing is as vital to people on life's journey as the federal highway system is to interstate travelers and commerce. Yet there are no realistic standards for providing basic social services in this country. State by state, our social service network has been built piecemeal, without bridges to give continuity. People traveling through the confusing traffic jam of social services find that highways dead-end in dirt paths; off-ramps are missing; programs are backlogged. The system is in perpetual gridlock, with funding for basic supports such as public schools and clinics declining as the demand for their services grows more intense.

All Americans have a stake in building the railing, and the participation of millions of people in grass-roots efforts signals the beginning of a new era of social rebuilding in our country. We need a plan that is cohesive and achievable—not piecemeal or grandiose. Four major pieces of the railing are outlined below:

CHILD DEVELOPMENT

America must invest more resources at the beginning of life. I propose the creation of a national children's trust fund to complement the Social Security trust fund.

The children's fund would ensure that every mother receives comprehensive nutrition and prenatal care; enhance child development for children in day-care centers and schools; and provide health care to all children. It would make Head Start available to all children at risk, and it would build on the experience of the Comprehensive Child Development Program to provide developmental aid for both mothers and children. For older children, it would provide developmental assistance to students, as in the Comer schools. It would encourage more states to adopt New Jersey's School-Based model of social services. It would help local efforts, like those in Sunset Park, Brooklyn, to build community around schools.

The start-up cost of the fund would be $15 billion a year—less than half of what Medicaire spends on terminal patients' care—a wise investment in young lives. This is the amount the National Commission on Children has proposed for additional programs to ensure adequate health, education, and family support for America's children.

FAMILY SUPPORT

The second stage of the railing should provide a secure environment for families. In a free society, families must have the right to define themselves.

The first step toward preserving family life is to make it illegal for any federal, state, or local government to force fathers like Eddie Baskin to leave home for their children to get assistance, and for any official to ask families like the Millers to divorce in order to qualify for health care.

The second step is for the government to back up families struggling to fulfill their responsibilites. In the average American family, both parents work outside the home; they need quality child care and family leave to fulfill dual roles as parents and workers. To withstand stresses that currently destroy one in two U.S. marriages, the railing must also provide family preservation services to preserve the hub of generations.

The third step is to prevent the predictable crisis of divorce from plunging children and single parents into poverty. The railing must include a national child-support assurance system that requires every absent parent to pay child support—or face federal penalties—and ensures every child a secure source of income. The start-up cost for a national child-support system is several billion dollars, but annually, $5 billion in child support is never collected. If effective, the system should pay for itself in reduced welfare costs.

HEALTH CARE FOR ALL

Americans need a railing of health care that begins before birth and attends to the needs of people at every stage of life's journey. A strong railing would focus on prevention, provide regular checkups, ensure medical treatments and hospitalization, allocate health resources where they can do the most good, and reduce waste caused by futile procedures. Universal health coverage would prevent patients from being denied care or forced into poverty to get it.

Health-care reform is high on President Clinton's agenda. Specific proposals, whether modeled on "managed competition," "pay or play," the "Oregon model," or the Canadian or German health system, all have virtues and flaws. The heated argument over whether the government or the private sector should be in charge of health care is just an excuse to do nothing. Both are already deeply involved; the key is to make them partners in creating a better system for all. I prefer to argue for principles rather than specific legislative plans, which may, at any rate, be overtaken by events.

The harmful experiences with government officials recounted in this book cause me to pay attention not to the promises of leaders and the grandiose provision of health plans, but rather to the realities that face people trying to get timely, adequate health care.

A railing of health care that would serve families like the Millers and Baskins would:

1. Be accessible to all Americans, regardless of insurance, employment, or preexisting health conditions, and without long waits or excessive eligibility barriers.
2. Cut health costs so that health care becomes affordable to individuals and the society as a whole.
3. Allocate care to people on a basis of medical need and efficacy of treatment, not level of profit.
4. Focus on prevention, from prenatal to hospice care, at all stages of life.
5. Provide full hospitalization, with deductibles on a sliding scale.
6. Pay for long-term home care and respite care for family caregivers.
7. Improve health and sex education and encourage people to make healthy life-style choices for their own well-being.
8. Organize the health-care system to integrate obstetrics, pediatrics, family medicine, and gerontology into a life-spanning railing, with continuity of care for people as they grow and age.

What will these reforms cost? This country currently spends $800 billion a year on health care, of which $200 billion is wasted on useless, ineffective, and bogus procedures, according to *Consumer Reports* magazine. If this money were saved and turned to good use, America could extend comprehensive care to 37 million uninsured Americans, without spending more than we do now. Canada, Germany, and Japan all spend less on health care than America does, and all manage to provide universal health coverage. If they can do it in their way, so can we design our own American system to fit our needs.

The underlying principle is that health care should no longer be a privilege for those who can afford it, but a right of all Americans.

SOCIAL SECURITY

The final section of the railing, Social Security, is the only one now in place. It is America's most successful social program, the most effective in alleviating poverty, and it has the strongest political support. But it has flaws that harm many pensioners, especially women.

The challenge is to reform Social Security without destroying it, to make the system more equitable for men and women, and to ensure that it remains viable for future generations.

One proposal to provide equity for the poorest pensioners—very old widows—is to impose a progressive tax on wealthy recipients who do not depend on Social Security for survival. This is controversial because it calls into question whether Social Security is a social insurance system or a welfare system for the elderly. In fact, it is both. Taxing the benefits of the wealthiest beneficiaries is an ethical way for this generation to provide more equitable benefits for its poorest members in their declining years.

The second challenge is to pass on an inheritance from the elderly to children. By taxing capital gains when someone dies and then decreasing estate tax exemptions from $600,000 to $300,000, the National Commission on Children estimates that nearly $8 billion in revenues could be collected. This inheritance alone would fund half of the children's trust fund proposed in this chapter.

The remaining challenge is to humanize the process of

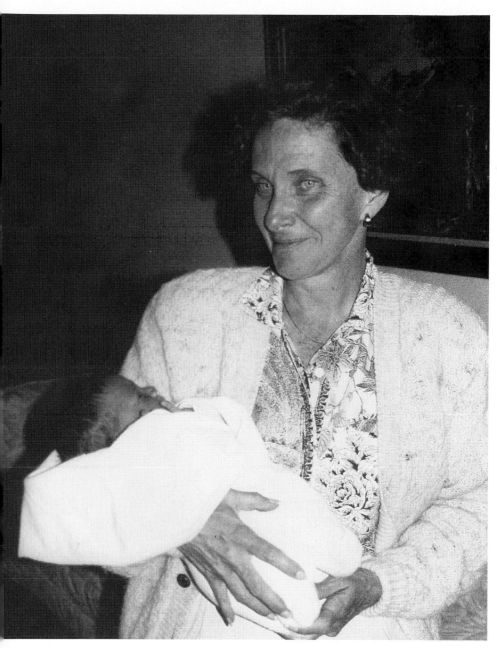

Jean Comer holding Kenya's "clean, healthy baby" in San Diego.
(Jonathan Freedman)

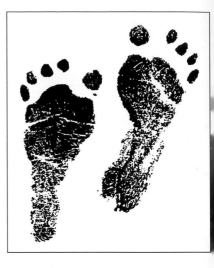

A.J.'s footprints (actual size at birth).

Cindy Miller holds her son, A.J., while Tim Miller cradles Nicholas at their home in Wabash, Indiana. (*The Journal-Gazette*, Fort Wayne, Indiana)

Boys using bedsprings as a trampoline in East New York.
(Jonathan Freedman)

Gayle Baskin in front of the public housing cottage where she lived while her husband was forced to sleep in the cemetary in Nashville, Tennessee.
(Jonathan Freedman)

Agin Shaheed and his students in San Diego's Public Advocate Program.
(Leonard Thompson)

Cheryl holds her
daughter, Kayla.
(Rod Huling)

Timothy learns computer-aided drafting at Focus: HOPE, Detroit, Michigan.
(Jonathan Freedman)

Claribel in front of the motel that she and her three siblings once used as a homeless shelter, Dover, New Jersey.
(Jonathan Freedman)

Mary Lou and her son
in Oak Ridge, Tennessee.
(Jonathan Freedman)

Nitza (*left*) and her counselor Myrna at the Citizens Advice Bureau, South Bronx, New York. (Jonathan Freedman)

Lee Sliwinski, his wife, daughter, and grandson, Wyandotte, Michigan.
(Jonathan Freedman)

Joe Allen Bennett, ailing from cancer, with his parents in Franklin, Tennessee.
(Mattie Sue Owens)

Christina Halkett in the room in the nursing home where she has lived since
1976. (*The Boston Globe*)

dying and give people with terminal illnesses more choices about their care. The overwhelming majority of senior citizens are in favor of living wills, documents in which they specify what treatments they do and do not want. The honoring of advance directives and the greater utilization of hospice services would save money wasted in futile and agonizing treatments at the end of life, and leave an inheritance for people at the beginning.

COST OF NEW PROGRAMS

What is the cost of additional programs to complete the railing? No federal commission has computed the cost of building a support structure from infancy to old age. The National Commission on Children, the Pepper Commission on health care, and other government bodies have estimated costs for building crucial pieces of the railing. Depending on whose numbers you use, a railing of child development, family support, and employer-based "pay or play" health insurance might cost between $15 billion and $60 billion a year—a throat-tightening range of expense in today's budget-conscious environment.

But the overall cost to the taxpayers would actually be far less: The extent of reductions would be in direct proportion to the effectiveness of preventive programs. The principle of prevention, shown by the dramatic cost-saving effect of prenatal care, goes for every stage of life. If a railing prevented only a fraction of the needless destruction and waste of lives of the status quo, it might save at least $15 to $60 billion each year.

The important thing is to begin building the railing now. Hard times need not deter us from positive action; in the depths of the Depression, President Roosevelt had the foresight to start the Social Security system. Piece by

215

piece, the railing may be built incrementally, with the initial investment beginning now and reaching completion by the year 2000.

With a conceptual framework of the railing in place, the money would not be adding to the labyrinth of social programs, but leading a way out.*

THE RAILING

A diagram of the railing stretching from infancy to old age would look like this:

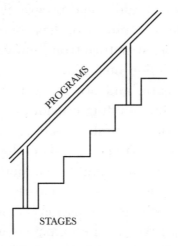

PROGRAMS

STAGES

* By jot and tittle, $60 billion equals the annual surplus being added to the Social Security trust fund to cope with the anticipated needs of the Baby Boom generation. The surplus is roughly equivalent to 1 percent of payroll taxes. Levying an additional 1 percent payroll tax—about $350 a year for a family earning $35,000—would build the railing from childhood to retirement. This would require only $7 a week for working Americans and would not jeopardize Social Security or take anything away from today's pensioners. Extending the railing would enable working people to pool their resources to provide services they desperately need today for their children, families, and health.

An alternative source of funding would be to raise taxes on the wealthiest Americans. If pre-Reagan tax rates were restored for the top tax bracket, this would raise more than $85 billion a year to complete the railing.

Again, events in Washington may overtake specific proposals. However, it will still be true that the cost of building the railing will reduce the waste of lives and build a healthier, more productive America.

This plan is offered as a preliminary blueprint, not a final working drawing. The potential drawbacks of the railing are significant: It is not a substitute for jobs that pay a living wage, nor for public assistance that is sufficient to bring people out of poverty. Neither is it a substitute for family and community, but rather a way of supporting them.

Although political conservatives will likely attack the railing as just another guise for a socialistic welfare state, it still would provide only a bare-bones system of supports—far less generous than our competitors in Western Europe and Japan.

Liberals may criticize it for failing to provide the hard cash necessary to raise people out of poverty by income transfers. But the key to the railing is to enable people to help themselves, not just depend on the government.

The answer to both camps is that only government can build critical sections of the railing, but the government alone cannot (indeed, should not) be the sole support for people ascending the stairs.

The cost of building a supportive social network is immense. I asked Eugene Steuerle, the former deputy assistant secretary of the Treasury for tax analysis (the highest economic tax official from the Reagan administration) if America could afford it.

"No doubt we have the resources to build the railing you describe," Steuerle, now a senior fellow at the Urban Institute in Washington, said in 1991. "As long as we're in a society with income growth, we have an increasing ability to build this railing. This whole thing that we don't have the resources is a myth. Arguing that the deficit prevents us from acting is like arguing that we can't act now because our actions prevent us from acting."

When Washington wants to act, it finds the money. In the midst of the biggest deficit in U.S. history, the Bush administration committed over $200 billion to bail out the thrift banks—enough to fund the railing for years.

The failure to build an effective support system will only magnify the destructive trends we see all about us. In 1960, before the first signs of family disintegration were noticed, fewer than 6 million American children lived in single-parent families. By 1990, that number nearly tripled to 16 million children. The number of children living with a never-married parent increased twentyfold during that period, from 243,000 children in 1960 to 4.9 million children in 1990.

During the 1980s, poverty rates for children climbed—from 16 percent in 1978 to 21 percent in 1990. As a result, America's child poverty rate was 10 times higher than in Sweden, seven times higher than in West Germany, and twice as high as in Canada and Australia.

Childhood deprivation foretells problems for America's children. One in five of our youngsters is born to poverty; half of America's children grow up in broken families; millions who attend underfunded schools will enter the workforce with inferior training, confronting a shrinking industrial job market. This same generation of children born in the eighties and nineties must contend with increasing economic competition from trade blocs in Europe and Asia. By mid-life, they will be saddled with the burden of supporting the retirement of the Baby Boom generation. If those workers can't compete internationally and can't support their elders domestically, there is a danger that the structure of our economic system could begin to collapse. Then it will no longer be a matter of people "falling through the cracks." America itself would plunge into poverty.

Building a railing to meet these challenges would be an enormous task, difficult beyond measure, politically perilous, economically costly, requiring great sacrifice. If the President of the United States pledged to build the railing, it would be less dramatic, perhaps, than President Kennedy's pledge to land on the moon, but accomplishing it would have a far greater impact on earth.

A vision of hope is valuable in a time of uncertainty. But the lives in this book also teach that there are no simple solutions, no guaranteed programs, no national agendas that work in all cases. Expectations must be set at real levels. Hopes that programs will solve all problems, that one victory will change everything, are likely to provoke disappointments that cause us to give up. Expectations that poor families will solve all their problems are unrealistic.

Yet there is movement on the stairs, tenuous and uneven, generally in an upward direction. In the midst of life's continuing challenges, the following sketches show where people are now on the stairs, one to three years after I first met them:

Kenya Williams, now thirty, has been clean of drugs for two years. Her fifteen-month-old son, Miles, is a healthy, twenty-pound, very active boy. His favorite word is *daddy*, but his real daddy is away in a residential drug rehabilitation program, so the men he looks up to are his grandfather and uncle. Kenya is reconciled with her parents, who are allowing her and Miles to live at home and giving them love and support. "I couldn't do it without them," she says.

Kenya is excelling in computer science at San Diego City College, where she has achieved a 3.3 grade point average. Her career goal is to become a software designer, but she will do programming, if necessary, to support Miles. She worries about the high mortality rate for young black men, and wishes out loud, "I hope to see him reach twenty-one." Her greatest fear is that she will go back on drugs and lose everything she has. Kenya struggles daily, saying: "I'm grateful to be clean."

The University of California San Diego Medical Center, where Kenya Williams's crack baby died in 1989, is admitting significantly fewer sick, "no-care" babies in 1992. The head nurse for the infant-care unit that is on the front line of the drug-baby epidemic says that increased funding for prenatal care, along with the successes of Options for Recovery and the opening of the Birth Place prenatal and delivery center, have begun turning the tide. Word is also out on the street that the university hospital performs drug testing for mothers who received no prenatal care, and consequently some drug mothers are delivering elsewhere.

Janine Dubina, the hospital's special infant-care director, praises the program that helped Kenya deliver her second baby free of drugs. "Options for Recovery has a significant impact for women who truly choose a different life-style," Janine says. "We're not getting as many sick babies. They're getting better care."

On a day in August 1992, there was only one no-care baby in the intensive care unit—a marked contrast to two years before, when the nursery was crowded with babies suffering from low birthweight, syphilis, and other preventable conditions stemming from lack of prenatal care.

California has increased spending on prenatal care despite its budget deficit, and the medical community has organized to encourage gynecologists to take poor patients. Even with these improvements, about 10 percent of the mothers who deliver in San Diego receive no prenatal care—with the immense cost of sick babies passed onto society.

At age three, A.J. Miller weighs only twenty-eight pounds, but has grown to be more than three feet tall. Cindy Miller is grateful that he has no brain damage, but she's frustrated that his fine-motor skills are lagging behind. A.J. is hyperactive, a condition heightened by theophylline, a drug he must take to aid his heartbeat and breathing. His occupational therapist says he is about six months behind his age group and estimates it will be two years before he catches up.

Cindy stays home in Wabash, Indiana, to take care of A.J., while husband Tim struggles with his carpet-cleaning business in the recession. Strapped, they have gone into debt to pay taxes. Only A.J. has health insurance. Cindy is terrified that if anyone else in the family falls ill, they may lose their home.

Cheryl, now twenty, and the interracial baby she bore as a single teenage mother, are doing well in Auburn, Washington. At three, Kayla is a vibrant, independent child who has advanced ahead of most others of her age. She receives developmentally sound child care at the Families First program while her mother is in college. With the support of the federally funded Comprehensive Child Development Program that helps both babies and their parents, Cheryl has finished her paralegal degree and is working toward a bachelor's degree in sociology at the University of Washington. She wants to be a probation officer and is volunteering at a juvenile detention center. Cheryl is engaged to a marine and plans a wedding six months before graduation. She serves as chairperson of the parent council advising Families First.

The Comprehensive Child Development experiment, in over twenty sites nationally, will not release general data until the federal government concludes its analysis of the pilot project after 1995. But Family First's ebullient director, Peg Mazen, has already applied for a $1.5 million grant from the state of Washington to serve additional clients. Her goal is to phase in state funding as the federal experimental project terminates in 1995—to make Families First a permanent program for needy families.

Cheryl thanks Families First and TAP, the high school program for teenage mothers, for giving her the foundation to believe in herself. "Just because you got pregnant, you're not a failure," she says.

Kevin Baskin, ten, the suicidally depressed Tennessee boy whose family couldn't afford psychiatric care, is finally receiving treatment at Murrell, a special school for learning-disabled children in Nashville. "He's getting better one minute and getting worse the next," says his mother. Gayle Baskin is thankful that he has stopped trying to commit suicide, but he still gets depressed and she has to watch over him constantly. She feels blessed that Kevin qualifies for Supplemental Security Income (SSI) and Medicaid for his learning disability and acute depression. The family now receives $602 in total monthly assistance, including Kevin's $422 SSI benefit. The increased money helped Gayle move her family out of the dangerous housing project into a $350-a-month rental home with a front yard and backyard. It is located in a quiet neighborhood where no gunshots ring out at night. Kevin is making new friends with the neighbors, climbing the big tree in the back yard. The Baskins now live close to their church, a source of continuing faith.

Eddie Baskin is no longer sleeping in the graveyard. He has a new job driving an armored bank truck. The Baskins are working out their marital difficulties, which began when the government of Tennessee forced Eddie to move out so his wife and children could receive public assistance. Federal SSI benefits do not require the spouse to live outside the home, and Eddie is now in the process of moving back with his wife and children. Gail's greatest hope is that her reunited family will be able to continue living in their new home and that Kevin will get better.

Claribel, twenty, the big sister who survived her mother's murder, has taken major steps forward to creating a stable life for her orphaned siblings and herself. With the continuing support of the School-Based Tiger RAP program in Dover, New Jersey, Claribel entered Morris County Community College in the fall of 1992 as a scholarship student in the school's new microcomputer program. She wakes up each weekday at 4 A.M. and works at a bakery until 9 A.M., when she begins her school day. In addition to taking care of her siblings, working, and going to school, Claribel is developing a deeper but not dependent relationship with her boyfriend. Carlos lives separately, but has taken the role of surrogate father and helps Claribel with the children and housework. Claribel wants to postpone wedding plans until she has graduated from college and has a full-time job.

The children are doing well, but tragedy still casts its shadow over their lives. Manny, seven, who witnessed his parents' murder-suicide, receives aid for his emotional disability and is enrolled in a special school. At first he rejected other men, but he has come to accept Claribel's boyfriend. Manny is no longer given to emotional outbursts and responds to love and discipline, but his psychiatrist says it may be two to seven years before he can cope with the tragedy.

Manuela, nine, is withdrawn and quiet. It's hard for her to talk about the death of her mother, and she is not doing particularly well in public school. Claribel is having her tested to see if she needs counseling or a special program.

Jorge, eighteen, has been befriended by a male teacher in high school. But he still lacks motivation, sleeps a lot, and Claribel feels he needs something to look forward to.

Claribel's struggle to build a better life for her family is not without constant challenges. The housing department tried to evict her after an inspector found she had bought new furniture, accusing her of having too much money. Her School-Based counselor, Kelly Gleason, had to intervene and show that Claribel borrowed $600 from the bank for the furniture and was paying it off with her earnings. "Without Tiger RAP, I wouldn't be doing what I am today," Claribel says. "They were like a family helping me with everything. In school, financially and emotionally, they were always there."

The School-Based program is expanding in New Jersey, where it now reaches 20,000 students. In the worst year of state budget cuts, the program went unscathed because of strong support and overwhelming evidence of its effectiveness. In one New Jersey high school where the program was tried, the dropout rate was reduced by two-thirds, suspensions by three-quarters, and teen pregnancies from 20 cases in 1989 to one case in 1991. School-Based was the winner of a national award for innovation from the Ford Foundation and Harvard's Kennedy School of Government, and it is now being replicated in Iowa and Kentucky.

Parts of the program are being adapted to California and Washington, D.C. Eventually, Ed Tetelman hopes to bring the School-Based concept of social services to children across the United States.

After helping save Boyle Heights from being torched in the L.A. riots, Father Boyle chose to take a one-year sabbatical from his Latino parish and youth center. The sabbatical would provide a chance for spiritual renewal for the priest, who buried dozens of parishioners murdered in gang violence. Concern about the effect of his leaving on the poor community was so high that word of his departure was front-page news in the *Los Angeles Times*. Later, the newspaper reported that, for undisclosed reasons, superiors in the Church had ordered Father Boyle not to return to the parish—a devastating blow to the people of Boyle Heights.

Susan Speir's teenage daughters in Los Angeles carry lasting scars from their father's abandonment of them when they were children. According to Susan, both daughters distrust men, and her eldest daughter, who was three when her father walked out, has had a hard time with relationships. A boyfriend beat her so badly that he put her in the hospital, but she didn't want to press charges against him.

Dedicated to helping other women gain child support, Susan continues to run SPUNK, a support group for single parents seeking child-support payments. She says that Los Angeles has 400,000 cases on file of failure to pay child support. Among them, only 35,000 of the parents are currently paying child support, Sue says bitterly. It's easy for absent parents to cross state lines to avoid being caught. They also receive payments under the table so not to report income to the government. Clearly, the child-support system is not working.

In Oak Ridge, Tennessee, ADFAC director Carol Siemens says that the fortunes of public housing neighbors Billie Jean and Mary Lou seem to have reversed. Harley's frustrations with life outside of prison erupted in outbursts of violence, and he reportedly beat up Billie Jean. Instead of suffering abuse passively—the way she had handled molestation as a child—Billie Jean left her husband. Meanwhile, one of her daughters was sexually molested by a man while staying the night at a friend's house. The accused molester was identified but never brought to justice. Although Harley lives apart from the family, he continues to pay child support. But Billie Jean's home phone has been disconnected, without a forwarding number.

Impoverished widow Mary Lou, whose children were undernourished, has unexpectedly remarried, once again to a man considerably older than she. He is a disabled coal miner who suffers from black lung disease and is living on a disability pension. She and her children have moved out of the housing project into his home. His black lung pension pays enough money for all of them to live on, and he has taken a fatherly interest in her children. The son with emotional problems is in a special education class. For as long as her husband's health lasts, Mary Lou's family seems secure. Her voice sounds grateful and happy.

Nitza, thirty-seven, the homeless mother who once sought help at the Citizens Advice Bureau in the South Bronx, still works full-time at the agency and has been promoted to a public policy position. As an associate member of the Bronx Welfare Advocacy Network, Nitza now sits at the conference table with officials from the New York Human Resources Administration, advising them on welfare policy. She is a board member of the National Welfare Rights Union, and co-founder of the Coalition for Welfare Rights of New York City. She is preparing to attend college and dreams of getting a professional degree to continue her work helping other welfare mothers.

But Nitza's travails as head of a family trapped in a crime-ridden poverty neighborhood continue.

Her seventeen-year-old daughter, Carmen, who suffers clinical psychosis, was impregnated by a thirty-two-year-old neighbor. Nitza accused the man of statutory rape, but the police never pressed charges. Nitza counseled her daughter to have an abortion, but the psychiatric center where the pregnant teenager was under treatment gave the minor a choice, and she delivered high-risk, premature twins. One suffers neurological disorders and the other is partially blind. Carmen was not able to deal with them and left home, so Nitza's mother is now raising the babies.

Yvette, twelve, who was a baby when Nitza put the children in foster care, is in the throes of teenage rebellion. When Nitza tried to discipline her for going out without permission, Yvette called child protection authorities and accused Nitza of child abuse. Nitza says the charges are trumped up and she never abused her daughter. She refused an offer to plea-bargain for a misdemeanor, and is angry at the authorities for not doing a thorough investigation before intervening heavy-handedly in her family. Nitza finally opted to place Yvette with another foster family, but before authorities came to pick her up, she ran away.

Her fourteen-year-old son, Raymond, is doing well, Nitza says, but she worries that he may follow the example of his drug-abusing father. Both he and her fourth daughter, Ada, are living at home; both are in counseling to cope with emotional problems stemming from being separated from their mother when she was homeless.

Nitza suffers the lingering legacy of three years on the streets, separated from her children in foster care. "They all knew I loved them," Nitza sighs. "I came twice a month and reassured them I loved them. We'd sing 'Old McDonald.'"

Nitza was able to overcome cycles of abuse and welfare dependency in her own life, to hold a steady job, and transform her pain into meaningful help for others. But she has not been able to protect her own children and grandchildren from further suffering, and the overwhelmed and underfunded public institutions that should be helping are often making things worse.

In Detroit, Timothy, thirty-one, the neglected child who watched his sister burn to death, graduated from Focus: HOPE and got a job as a computer-aided design operator. The work Timothy accomplished is impressive: He helped design an A-frame control arm for Ford vehicles, and a transfer machine for couplings for oil-well drills.

But after eleven months and two pay raises, Timothy's company lost a contract and he was laid off. He is left with a pile of bills and four children to raise. He can't afford a phone, so he uses a beeper to return calls. This draws suspicion that he is a drug dealer, although he has steered away from drugs since entering Focus: HOPE. The son Timothy fathered as a teenager is now fourteen years old and lives with his father. He is an honors student in a so-called compact school. By arrangement with a local university, the school offers those who graduate with at least a 3.0 average a guaranteed university scholarship. Timothy now hopes his son will go on to college.

"Focus: HOPE taught me self-discipline, that I can accomplish what I want to do," Timothy says. His teacher at the machinist's training institute is still involved, helping him look for new jobs.

Erica Wright, who founded the West Side Cultural and Athletic Club in Detroit, has both tragic and hopeful news to report: Three of the young men who shared their dreams and fears with me on a midnight tour of their burned-out neighborhood have died violently in the past two years. Two of the children are now living on the street.

But one youth in the group won a trip to China for his academic and musical accomplishments. Another young man recently graduated from college and landed a high-paying job with the Internal Revenue Service.

Erica, who also runs a program for seniors, says Detroit recently turned over a senior center to house homeless families. The center has been taken over by drug addicts who kick in the doors and rape elderly women.

Erica feels she's fighting a one-woman battle against drugs, violence, and neglect. She desperately needs funding to rehab a building and provide transportation for seniors.

"I've got fourteen kids in college and another fourteen who've graduated," she says proudly. "But ninety percent of the young kids in the club have addicted or alcoholic parents. When these abused kids act out in school, they put them on medication because it's cheaper than sending them to a social worker. The kids are walking around like zombies . . . "

Erica remains committed to stay in her neighborhood, where she runs the summer Olympics for hundreds of Detroit children every year.

Permanently dislocated Firestone steelworker Lee Sliwinski, fifty-one, is driving a taxi and bringing home $200 a week to keep his family afloat. His wife has suffered two heart attacks and requires medication, but the Sliwinskis have no health insurance and have to pay for her prescriptions with cash. With bills for rent, utilities, and food consuming everything Lee earns, they are barely making it and can't afford to pay for medical checkups for Mrs. Sliwinski's heart condition. Lee is still hoping for a job in the automotive industry; his son-in-law has put his name on a hiring list for an auto seatcover factory, but it may be months before it opens up, if ever.

Despite Lee's experience, the situation in Detroit is not hopeless for all dislocated workers. The Job Connection program in Livonia is successful in finding new jobs for workers dislocated by plant closures. After eighteen closures in the area, the Job Connection has helped nearly 1,100 dislocated workers make the transition to employment or education.

Today, 750 workers have new jobs, and another 175 are completing educational programs to upgrade skills or gain new ones. Dislocated hospital workers who were making $6 an hour are now earning $9 an hour as nurse trainees. But autoworkers earning $15 an hour were forced to go back to work at $9 to $11 an hour. Their new jobs are as medical assistants, accountants, and computer operators. The program, funded by the federal Economic Dislocated Worker Adjustment Assistance Act (EDWAAA), averages an 80 to 90 percent success rate in finding new jobs for people who are enrolled, says program director Becky Nordstrom. But few slots are available: In Michigan, only 7 percent of laid-off workers are able to use the program's resources, and people like Lee Sliwinski are not eligible.

Early retirement didn't suit Jean Comer, fifty-six. After leaving Options for Recovery to take care of her sick mother, Jean is back in the trenches, doing drug counseling at a private hospital, one on one. Her fear is that people who are helping others will believe the media and politicians that the economy is "going to hell, nothing works, and there's no hope"—and will give up. "It's not true," she says. Her greatest hope lies in the world being healed through self-help programs. "There's nothing more exciting than treatment," she says, caring for her mother, her family, and her clients. Jean has no plans to retire.

Harriet Houston, Jean Comer's mother, was hospitalized for complications arising from emphysema and failing health. Her condition was listed as critical and doctors told Jean not to expect her mother to survive. Harriet passed away in January 1993.

Just when Jean's life began to settle back to normal, her husband, Stuart Comer, was diagnosed with liver cancer in the spring. "I feel overwhelmed," Jean says, after returning with Stuart from an exhausting day of oncology tests at the hospital. "Someone's got to do something about the crisis in health care."

Mollie Orshansky, the creator of The Poverty Line, has

retired from government. She says, "Why don't we stop doing research on the right poverty number and do something about poverty?"

Christina Halkett is ninety-four, beginning her seventeenth year in a nursing home. Despite multiple ailments lingering from a stroke, broken hip, gallbladder operation, intestinal surgery, and a sprained back that leaves her in constant pain, she's still on the go, advocating the rights of nursing home residents. The Scottish-born seamstress who refused to be silenced on her first day in the nursing home dining room in 1976 recently spoke out to Massachusetts governor Weld, condemning the cuts of personal allowances to nursing home residents.

"My nineties are very active," says Christina. "I have still more things to help complete." She serves on the mayor's advisory council, the board of directors of the elder activists' group LIFE, and is president of the Resident's Council at the Bostonian Nursing Care Center.

When a doctor recently asked her for advance directives if she fell terminally ill, Christina told him: "I'm old and have lived long enough. I wouldn't like to be operated on again. I don't want to be brought back and suffer more. I'd like to let go."

Christina believes that the elderly should give a legacy to children. She wants all children to grow up knowing they are needed on this earth. She remembers her own childhood early in the century, when she fell and cracked her skull against a rock on the cliffs of Rosehearty, Scotland. There were no X rays in those days and the skull fracture injured her brain. For years, she was considered dull, unable to study or work. Her recovery was aided by a local grocer who saw the child being neglected.

He told her he believed in her, and challenged her to cro-
chet a difficult pattern. After she painstakingly accomplished it nearly a year later, he gave her praise. Once
someone believed in her, Christina says, she gained the
ability to believe in and fend for herself. She will never
forget others in need, because she knows what it is to be
neglected.

An active member of LIFE, Christina stays in close
contact with Ed Alessi and tries to make things more
pleasant for her fellow nursing home residents. Looking
back on her long life, she believes that what's most
important is to have faith and hope. "People need help at
every age," she says, looking forward to what she can do
today.

If these ordinary people who suffered tragedies and
deprivation can take steps forward, so can America.
Programs like Options for Recovery, the Birth Place,
Families First, the Comer model, School-Based Tiger
RAP, SPUNK, Focus: HOPE, the Job Connection, LIFE,
and hospice care are building a railing for Americans at
every stage of life.

These programs are only a small sampling of the thousands operating in communities across America.
Wherever I traveled, people showed me vital helping projects, and I regret not having more time or space to docu-
ment other innovative programs. We are a nation of
social innovators, yet few Americans have access to the
wealth of experience from other communities. A central
information bank of programs and methods would be a
national asset, aiding the cross-fertilization of practical
ideas.

Further, these programs have much in common: They
are nurtured by the grass roots and by the government;

they help people help themselves; they are not anonymous, but require a personal connection; they provide support during difficult life transitions; their methods are effective for poor people as well as for the middle class; they build self-confidence; they give back to their communities.

Still, the reach of such programs is too small to cope with the crushing volume of social destruction in this country. Government is needed as an active partner with grass-roots efforts in building the railing.

I have been fortunate to meet people who have made it through difficulties that I could not have imagined, and they taught me the value not of rugged individualism, but of tenacious relationships. At times I concluded that the ultimate value of a particular program was not in its overt reason for being, but for the fact that it provided a way for two people—one in need of help and another wanting to help—to form a bond transforming both their lives.

If there is a railing to help people, it will be made up of not just government programs or private efforts but of human hands. It takes money, organization, and laws to maintain a social structure, but none of it works if there are not opportunities for people to meet and help each other along the way. Social responsibility comes down to something simple—the ability to respond.

With committed leadership, our government may regain its ability to respond, and the private sector may become a better social partner. Ordinary people may take personal responsibility for their own kin, and make our government more responsive to all. But the most basic level of response is not governmental; it is intimate—one on one, neighbor to neighbor, family to family, community by community, hand by hand, until the railing is within our grasp.

The stairs are steep and perilous. At the bottom lurks despair that nothing can be done. At the top lies hope, not of easy solutions, but of difficult choices. The risk of failing to help people climb upward is outweighed by the danger of standing by helplessly while more people fall. All journeys begin by taking a first step.

INDEX

INDEX

INDEX

INDEX

INDEX

Jonathan Freedman was born in 1950 and grew up in Denver, Colorado, where he attended the public schools. He graduated Phi Beta Kappa from Columbia College in 1972, winning the Cornell Woolrich Writing Prize. His columns on social issues have been featured in *The New York Times*, the *Los Angeles Times*, and the *San Diego Tribune*. He was awarded a Pulitzer Prize for Distinguished Editorial Writing in 1987. His 1990 articles on foster children drew the attention of the National Commission on Children. Thus he began a three-year journey across America, researching and writing *From Cradle to Grave*. He lives with his wife, Maggie Locke, daughter Madigan, and son Nick in San Diego, California.